A
UNITED
IRELAND

A UNITED IRELAND

WHY UNIFICATION IS INEVITABLE

AND HOW IT WILL

COME ABOUT

KEVIN MEAGHER

Biteback Publishing

This paperback edition published in Great Britain in 2022 by
Biteback Publishing Ltd, London

Copyright © Kevin Meagher 2016, 2022

Kevin Meagher has asserted his right under the Copyright, Designs and Patents
Act 1988 to be identified as the author of this work.

ISBN 978-1-78590-665-7

10 9 8 7 6 5 4 3 2 1

A CIP catalogue record for this book is available from the British Library.

Set in Kepler

Printed and bound in Great Britain by
CPI Group (UK) Ltd, Croydon CR0 4YY

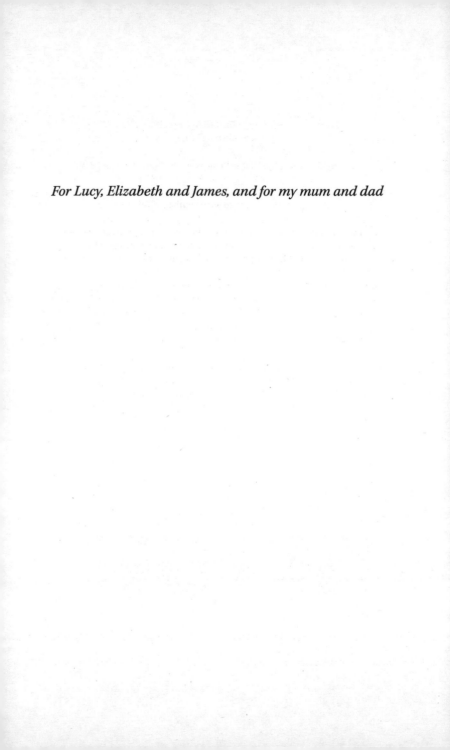

For Lucy, Elizabeth and James, and for my mum and dad

AUTHOR'S NOTE

Undoubtedly, this book will divide opinion. For every person who finds themselves in agreement with the arguments I set out, there will be others who strongly disagree.

The point, however, is to generate debate. To open up a discussion that has lain dormant for too long. To set out the truth as I see it. Others may have theirs.

But what is surely beyond contention is that Brexit, the ongoing threat of a Scottish breakaway and the growth of provincial English centres of power present very real challenges to Northern Ireland's place in the United Kingdom. Quite apart from the compelling empirical evidence that Irish unity now makes overwhelming economic sense.

In the time-honoured tradition, any omissions or inaccuracies over subsequent pages remain entirely my own.

CONTENTS

INTRODUCTION

It is five years since I wrote the first edition of this book. It feels like another world and much has happened in that time. I had just completed my first draft of the manuscript as Brexit occurred. The necessary second draft required me to process the biggest change in British political and economic life in a generation in real time. A political 'Big Bang' event, epic in its scale, dispersing debris across the political universe. Even now, the full implications of that decision have yet to be felt. Back in the summer of 2016, though, it was clear that it would alter everything, and that the effects felt in Northern Ireland would be greatest of all.

There had been warnings during the referendum campaign that the border between the British and Irish states – stretching 310 miles along the north-easternmost counties of Ireland – would present its own problems. A hard land border would be disastrous. A betrayal of the freedoms won by the Good Friday Agreement, which included an open border. Why put that at risk? John Major and Tony Blair, emeritus British Prime Ministers both, went to Northern Ireland during the campaign and said as much. No one was really listening, though. Brexit was, and is, chiefly an English phenomenon that was driven by concerns about mass immigration and a pervasive, but ill-defined, sense of malaise about the direction of the country. A yearning for old certainties. What the writer David Goodhart incisively referred to as a split between the people from 'anywhere', who embraced personal autonomy and consumerism, and the people from 'somewhere', who instead prided tradition, certainty and place. In the Brexit argot, the former group were ardent remainers, citizens of the world, instinctively socially liberal, at ease with societal and economic change. The latter were staunch leavers, social conservatives, unhappy by the pace of change and uncomfortable with where things were heading.

It sounds trite, but no one in the Westminster village entertained serious doubts about the result. All the main parties were campaigning to remain in the EU. There was an assumption baked into the campaign that voters would come round in the end. Better the devil they knew. Some might flirt with leaving but would not, ultimately, slip the leash of party allegiance. And if that did not quite do it, figures outside politics were urging them to remain. If David Cameron could not persuade voters, then perhaps David Beckham could. The view, then, was that the centre ground of British politics would not yield to what they regarded to be the anti-EU nutty fringe – romantic Tory nationalists (invariably English) and the remnants of the hard left, who still saw the EU as a 'capitalists' club'. They were roundly beaten in 1975, during the last referendum on the UK's membership of the EU, and the same would happen again in 2016. At any rate, this was the script. Brexit might have been an iceberg to these modern-day executives of the White Star Line, but it could not sink the European ideal.

Ultimately, the remain campaign capsized, and the result has been a source of contention ever since. Brexit was carried by 52 per cent to 48 per cent – narrow, but clear enough. Disaggregate it, though, and the row intensifies. In Scotland, 62 per cent voted to remain, reviving separatist demands following the 2014 independence referendum, where 45 per cent of Scots voted to leave the UK. Just two years later and they now had a fresh reason for demanding a second attempt.

In Northern Ireland, 56 per cent of voters chose to stay in the European Union. Again, the result has been a fillip for those demanding a border poll – the colloquial term for a referendum on Northern Ireland's constitutional position. Indeed, hardly a week goes by without someone from the non-Unionist parties pointing out that there is no mandate for Brexit in Northern Ireland. But this was a national referendum. There are no opt-outs for constituent parts of the UK. The result stands, as, indeed, do the implications. But were Northern Ireland to join the Irish Republic, readmission to the European Union would be automatic.

This has created a new and compelling argument for Irish unity. The benefits of EU membership are considerable, not least the €710 million in funding that Northern Ireland received each year. There are not many people from 'anywhere' in Northern Ireland – national identity is massively important for both Unionists and Irish Nationalists – however, there are many younger people who appear to be moving beyond the confines of this binary choice, looking outwards with optimism, who deplore the implications of Brexit. Might this group – particularly those from a Protestant–Unionist background – now tip the balance? Any vote on Irish unity now has an implicit second question: 'Do you want to rejoin the EU?' Could this group combine with farmers and business owners to vote for a united Ireland on purely utilitarian grounds? Do the benefits of a single Irish state within the EU now outweigh the costs? Are jobs, prosperity and the opportunities they bring more important than tradition and identity? While politics is about voting for the things you want to see happen, it is also about accepting the things you can live with.

At least initially, the Democratic Unionists were happy with the Brexit result. Their reductive thought process was that anything that made Northern Ireland less European also made it less Irish. Perhaps it seemed like that in the immediate aftermath; alas, for them, that is hardly how things have panned out. As I write, Unionists across the spectrum, from harrumphing grandees like David Trimble through to Loyalist corner boys, petrol bombs in hand, are muttering darkly about the Northern Ireland Protocol. This is the part of Boris Johnson's Brexit Withdrawal Agreement that ensures there is no hard border across the island of Ireland by checking goods and collecting customs at the ports instead, creating, in effect, a border in the Irish Sea.

So, Brexit represents an accelerant poured over the dry tinder of a host of underlying factors that were already pushing us towards Irish unification. The effects of Brexit – both political and economic – now intersect with the slow, grinding demographic changes that are set to see a further decline in the share of Northern Ireland's population that identifies as Protestant when the 2021 census reports. We then have an assembly election in May 2022 in which Sinn Féin may well top the poll, depriving Unionists of the role of First Minister in the process. (We have already seen a Sinn Féin surge in the south, winning the popular vote and coming within a seat of being the largest party in Dáil Éireann in the 2020 Irish general election.) Meanwhile, a raft of opinion polls have shown that support for Irish unity is growing, fuelling media coverage, both at home and around the world, speculating that Northern Ireland's future is now time-limited.

Over on the other side of the Irish Sea, supporters of independence have a majority in the Scottish Parliament, adding to the likelihood that there will be a second referendum there. Indeed, some Scottish independence campaigners have cited the Good Friday Agreement and a provision contained therein that a border poll cannot be held until seven years have elapsed from the previous one. It is a valuable and timely legal precedent, given Scotland's first independence referendum was in September 2014.

How will Unionists respond to these symbolic changes? Having seen Northern Ireland created to lock in a Protestant–Unionist ascendancy, how will it feel to them when that advantage is gone? What will they make of having a

Sinn Féin First Minister in charge of their 'wee country', especially if the party is also in power in Dublin at the next Irish general election? If Scotland leaves the UK, is there even any point in Northern Ireland remaining? Unionism, it seems, cannot break its losing streak. In chess, they call it 'zugzwang'. The losing player cannot turn things around. Every move weakens their overall position. The game is irretrievable.

*　　*　　*

A second edition is an invitation for the author to wallow in self-congratulation or to lament their folly. Like the curate's egg, my arguments back in 2016 were good in parts. The overall shape of my contention that Irish unification is inevitable remains intact, representing, as it does, a realistic and evidence-based proposition. Many will still cleave towards it because they consider it the righting of a historical injustice, but the issue is now also a sensible, practical and workable response to the times we are in – and this will entice many more to support it.

Over the past five years, the chatter about a border poll has become incessant. Campaign groups. Blogs. Podcasts. Events. Conferences. The debate, so long a marginal concern among Republicans, has moved centre-stage. A self-confident 'civic Nationalist' community leads the charge. People from business, professional life, charities and the arts are holding the ring on the discussion. The subject is a constant source of speculation among columnists, writers and broadcasters. (Since the publication of the first edition of this book, I must have conducted nearly 200 interviews about the subject, mostly with British and international broadcasters.)

As with the first edition, I am not setting out to provide the reader with a definitive history of Northern Ireland or the Troubles. Where I have made historical references, I have done so to illuminate a point. Clearly, when delving into the political affairs of Ireland, it is impossible for historical events not to play a significant part. Quite unavoidably, they soak onto every page, serving as context for the present and, all too often, a warning to the future.

Nor have I embarked on a work of political science. Northern Ireland has an erudite community of academics who pore over every event and nuance with diligence and expertise, with various sub-academic fields analysing the conflict. (Northern Ireland, with its idiosyncratic politics and troubled history, must be one of the most studied places on earth.) So, my intention is not to compete with the scholars. This book is intended to be an extended political argument. The aim is to raise questions that have been unsaid and unheard (and perhaps, even, unthought) in British politics for too long. I am trying to encourage a discussion about the most elemental issues in relation to Northern Ireland. Why are we still there? Will we ever leave? What are the circumstances that could propel us to do so? And what arrangements would we put in place instead?

And when I use the royal 'we' I mean Britain, or, more precisely, the British political class. This is a book about British politics. I am trying to assess the issues involved for what they mean for the British public and British public debate. Physically, socially and politically remote from the rest of the UK, and unviable as an economic entity in its own right, Northern Ireland's endurance for 100 years is merely testament to the indolence of a British political class that has been content to keep the place at arm's length whenever possible. A somewhat anomalous response given that the governance of Ireland and latterly Northern Ireland is probably the longest-running fault line in British politics. Indeed, the 'Irish question' (or, more often, the 'Irish problem') has dogged British politics, in one form or another, since at least the time of the 1800 Act of Union and the abolition of the Irish Parliament (if not for centuries before that), as the English crown and then the British state struggled – and invariably failed – to establish a popular mandate to govern the Irish. It is a question/problem that has rolled on into the modern age. During the last three decades of the twentieth century, it took the form of the Northern Ireland 'Troubles' (an epic piece of understatement for what amounted to a major secessionist uprising that cost the lives of 3,600 people) and although the past twenty years have seen intensive efforts to secure a devolved local settlement via the Good Friday Agreement, the constitutional status of Northern Ireland remains moot.

How could it not? British–Irish relations over much of the past millennium are a grisly tale of invasion, subjugation, ethnic cleansing, famine, disease, insurrection, counter-insurrection, retreats, partial victories and brooding stalemates. The province of Northern Ireland was created as a back-foot political compromise to split the difference between Republicans vying for national self-determination and Loyalists determined to have their identity and local hegemony rewarded.

Yet here we are, a century on, still in possession of the north-east corner of the island of Ireland – six counties of the historical province of Ulster – long past the point when there was any rational reason to remain. Rational, certainly, from the perspective of the British public. We have paid a heavy price, in both blood and treasure, for the failures of successive governments to oversee an orderly retreat from our oldest colony, a faraway land of which we know and seemingly care little. Now, two decades' worth of incremental political progress since the Good Friday Agreement is creating space where the long-term future of Northern Ireland can and should be openly discussed. We should seize the chance.

This book is a modest attempt to contribute to that debate. It will explore the historical context – how we have ended up where we are and why – before moving on to discuss how different Northern Ireland is to the rest of the UK; the role of economics in driving an all-Ireland future; the mood of the Irish Republic towards the question of unity; how the once-difficult relationship between Britain and Ireland has been transformed in recent years, providing a stable context for any change of sovereignty over the north; and it will offer an examination of the scenarios in which British political elites will be presented with a compelling case for Irish unity in the years to come, whether or not they choose to drive the agenda.

Kevin Meagher
November 2021

CHAPTER ONE

WHY WE ARE WHERE
WE ARE

It is quite impossible to write anything about Ireland without providing the reader with a historical precis. The trouble comes in deciding where to begin. There is so much history, so much context and so much political strife that it's comparable to explaining *Coronation Street* from the very beginning to a visiting Martian. Do we start with Strongbow? The Flight of the Earls? The Ulster Plantation? Cromwell? The suspension of the Irish Parliament? Wolfe Tone? The Fenians? Easter 1916? The War of Independence? Partition? The Irish Civil War? The sheer scale of it, to the uninitiated, which, in this case, is pretty much everyone in Britain, is bamboozling, with personalities, references and terms that are entirely unfamiliar. But it all matters. Each tumultuous event in Irish history, those mentioned above and dozens more besides, feed into one another, becoming symbiotic as one failed uprising against British rule simply inspires a repeat event. Each atrocity committed by the British state resulting in a backlash. Each rising being put down in brutal fashion. Historical grievances echo down the generations.

The fraught relationship between Britain and Ireland dates from the twelfth-century Norman invasion, beginning a sequence of rebellions, truces, stalemates, repressions and further rebellions that stretches into the modern era. The ambitious English King Henry II set foot in Ireland in 1171, but, although he secured bases in the east of Ireland, he did not manage to dominate the country. A century later, a Gaelic revival undermined this Norman conquest, aided by military victories for the native Gaels and the impact of the Black Death (which hit the Normans harder as they lived in towns while the rural Irish were more sparsely populated). England's grip over Ireland weakened and was reduced to the fortified parts of Dublin on the east coast known as the Pale, with its writ not running in the rest of the country ('beyond the Pale').

Under Henry VIII, there was a more concerted attempt to force Ireland's submission. Wary of the country being used as a backdoor to strike against England, Henry prosecuted a typically bloody campaign to centralise control under the Crown but was less successful in converting the native Irish to Protestantism. In order to consolidate his advances (and to avoid a similar fate to the Normans), lands were confiscated and a loyal garrison from England and Scotland would be brought to Ireland as part of the policy of 'plantation'. To bolster this new Protestant ascendancy in Ireland, a series of Penal Laws were introduced with the intention of killing off Catholicism altogether. They included a ban on Catholics sitting in the Irish Parliament, voting, practising law or serving as officers in the army or navy. Catholics were not allowed their own schools, or to send their children abroad to be educated. They could not marry Protestants and any priest who conducted such a ceremony faced death for his trouble. No Catholic could own a horse with a value of more than £5. Ingeniously, this law allowed a Protestant the right to buy any horse from any Catholic for that amount. The philosopher Edmund Burke described the system of Penal Laws as 'a machine of wise and elaborate contrivance, as well fitted for the oppression, impoverishment and degradation of a people, and the debasement in them of human nature itself, as ever proceeded from the perverted ingenuity of man'.

It's fair to say the Tudors left their mark on Ireland. In

English folklore, Sir Walter Raleigh is famed for the apocryphal tale of his chivalry, laying his cloak over a puddle for Elizabeth I to walk across. In Irish history, he is remembered as the English officer responsible for the massacre of 700 Spanish and Italian troops at the Siege of Smerwick in County Kerry in 1580. The soldiers, part of a papal force sent to assist the Irish nobles in resisting English rule, found themselves cut off and surrendered. Despite assurances to the contrary, and with the exception of a few officers, every man was killed.

Throughout the sixteenth and seventeenth centuries, English control of Ireland waxed and waned. One of the periodic bouts of rebellion led to the creation of the Irish Catholic Confederation, a seven-year period between 1642 and 1649 during which Irish nobles and the Catholic Church governed their own affairs through an assembly in Kilkenny. This flame of freedom was snuffed out when Oliver Cromwell began his conquest of Ireland in 1649. There is surely no figure in British and Irish history that so divides opinion in these isles. For the Irish, Cromwell is a fiend. An ethnic cleanser. A tyrant.

His notoriety was well earned. Landing in Ireland in 1649 with a force of 20,000 troops, Cromwell crushed all opposition before him, ordering the execution of more than 3,500 men, women and children loyal to King Charles I in Drogheda. The bloodlust continued in Wexford and a similar massacre ensued. Shortly after, word of Cromwell's atrocities spread, and opposition crumbled. This allowed him to seize the assets of the Catholic Church and sack its churches and monasteries. Catholic landowners were dispossessed and forcibly relocated to Connaught, Ireland's westernmost province (and, in agricultural terms, its least propitious). 'To Hell or to Connaught' was the choice. Cromwell's officers were paid in confiscated land, which many sold to the English and Scottish gentry, creating a class of absentee landlords. To top it off, Cromwell sold off defeated soldiers, women and children, exiling them to the West Indies.

The Restoration of the Monarchy in 1660 under Charles II brought little relief for the Irish. The one thing uniting Roundhead and Cavalier, parliamentarian and monarchist, was utter contempt for the Irish. In 1685, James II came to the throne. As a convert to Catholicism, Protestants feared the emergence of a Catholic restoration. Lord Danby, leader of the Whigs, encouraged James's son-in-law, the Dutch Prince William of Orange, to rise up against him. James was forced to flee to France before heading for Ireland in the hope of rallying support there to regain his throne. In 1690, his Jacobite army faced William's at the river Boyne in County Meath in southern Ireland. Outnumbered and outclassed by William's professional soldiers, James was defeated, again taking refuge in France from his estranged son-in-law. (Reliving this event remains the high point of the Orange Order's annual calendar.) William was eventually halted at Limerick by the Irish general Patrick Sarsfield, who forced William to agree to terms and in exchange agreed to disband his own army. The Treaty of Limerick of 1691 was to see religious freedom and the rights of the native Irish restored, while Sarsfield's army went into exile, forming brigades in many continental armies (somewhere in the region of 500,000 Irishmen – so-called 'wild geese' – would do the same over the next century, denied, by the Penal Laws, the right to serve in the English army). Sarsfield kept his part of the bargain. The English Parliament, however, did not.

By the late eighteenth century, only 5 per cent of Irish land was owned by Catholics, even though they made up three-quarters of the population. The ongoing and unjust effects of the Penal Laws led to a further rebellion. The Society of United Irishmen, led by Theobald Wolfe Tone, a Kildare lawyer, took inspiration from the American War of Independence and the French Revolution to champion a non-sectarian, independent Irish Republic, uniting 'Catholic, Protestant and Dissenter'. His call found a ready audience among Catholics but also Presbyterians (who were also subject to the Penal Laws, although not as harshly dealt with as Catholics). A rising in 1798 led by Tone was eventually put down and Prime Minister William Pitt moved to abolish the Irish Parliament and make Ireland part of the United Kingdom. The Act of Union became law in 1801. For his part, Tone is still revered as a theorist-martyr, providing an intellectual lodestar for contemporary Irish Republicans who seek to emulate his call for national self-determination on the basis of equality and liberty for all.

In 1823, another young lawyer tried different tactics. Daniel O'Connell formed the Catholic Association to campaign for an end to the Penal Laws and to improve the lot of impoverished tenant farmers. It soon became a mass movement, advocating non-violence, successfully fusing together the peasant Irish and the Catholic Church. The association began to win a series of parliamentary by-elections and, sensing the increasing political danger, Prime Minister Arthur Wellesley, the Duke of Wellington, introduced a Catholic Relief Bill in 1829, removing most of the institutionalised discrimination facing Catholics in both Ireland and Britain. At the same time, however, he introduced legislation to remove the franchise from many small farmers – the bedrock of the association's support.

As a pioneer of non-violent, mass mobilisation to secure political change, O'Connell – 'the Liberator' – next turned his efforts to repealing the Act of Union itself, with a series of 'monster meetings' at historical sites across the country. These were gatherings in the hundreds of thousands, culminating in a meeting in Cashel which up to a million people were said to have attended. A larger gathering still, planned for Tara, was banned by the authorities. Given O'Connell had been careful to keep his activities within the law, he decided to cancel the meeting, and, now aged seventy, political power drained away from him and toward more militant efforts for national self-determination.

Throughout the nineteenth century, efforts to obtain Irish freedom oscillated between constitutional agitation and attempts to remove Britain by force. From the mid-nineteenth century onwards, Irish affairs began to feature heavily in British politics (owing to the scrapping of the Irish Parliament and the presence of Irish MPs in the House of Commons). In 1844, there was a nine-day 'great debate' in the House of Commons on a motion put forward by Lord John Russell on the proposition that 'Ireland is occupied not governed'. The motion was defeated but the symbolism that Ireland was a place apart, a perennial problem that needed resolving, was founded in British politics. The 'Irish question' was born.

British politics was going through a relatively progressive phase at the time, but as the historian D. G. Boyce put it: 'The British belief in reasonable government, consensus and fair play, even if dismissed as typical of hypocritical Albion, could and did prove embarrassing to a British government bent on enforcing "firmness" in Ireland.'[1]

If parliamentarians thought Ireland was a problem in 1844, the following year would reveal just how big the problem was. So began *An Gorta Mor* – 'the Great Hunger' – a famine that would, over coming years, ravage Ireland, decreasing its population by a quarter, leaving a million souls to die terrible deaths from starvation and typhoid, while as many more were forced to emigrate. (Indeed, many put the numbers in both instances higher.) The virulent potato blight, *Phytophthora infestans*, carried on the wind and washed down into the soil, turned the potato crop, the staple diet of the peasant Irish, into putrid mush. Given the model of agrarian capitalism in Ireland, with its absentee English landlords and compartmentalised plots of land, the hardy potato was the only realistic crop that could be grown by subsistence farmers.

The effects of the blight were immediate and severe. When it came, help was partial and inadequate. The civil servant in charge of the relief effort, Sir Charles Trevelyan, an evangelical Christian and ardent disciple of laissez-faire, believed that 'the judgement of God sent the calamity to teach the Irish a lesson'. Such was the famine's scale that *The Times* remarked that 'a Celtic Irishman' would become 'as rare in Connemara as is the Red Indian on the shores of Manhattan'. The Lord Lieutenant of Ireland, George Villiers, the Earl of Clarendon (whose descendant Theresa Villiers was David Cameron's Northern Ireland Secretary), wrote to Prime Minister Lord John Russell beseeching him to intervene and avert this 'policy of extermination'.

This was British 'firmness' in action. The Irish had brought this on themselves and could not expect Britain to bail them out. Help, when it came, had strings attached. The Church of Ireland offered food aid to those who would renounce their Catholicism. 'Taking the soup' became the insult aimed at those who did. Queen Victoria offered the trifling amount of £1,000 worth of relief. Hearing about the plight of the Irish, the Sultan of the Ottoman Empire offered £10,000, only to have the British government ask him to reduce it so it did not embarrass the Queen. (The story goes that he still sent three ships laden with food aid surreptitiously.) In an equally remarkable gesture of international solidarity, the Native American Choctaw tribe raised money for the starving Irish.

As displaced people themselves, they empathised with the 'Trail of Tears' the Irish now found themselves on.

The memory of those years, the sheer scale of death and suffering, as well as the dislocation inflicted on that generation of Irish people, was seared into the collective memory of all subsequent generations. Of course, this being Ireland, it was not the first time the people had been left to starve by their English masters. The same thing had happened a century earlier. In 1740–41, famine was responsible for the deaths of a fifth of the population. Extreme cold and wet weather destroyed the grain harvests as well as the potato crop. To paraphrase Karl Marx, in Ireland, history repeats itself, the first time as tragedy and the second time as tragedy.

The rest of the nineteenth century is zipped between political attempts and militaristic forays to achieve independence via the ballot box, or by the musket. The Irish Parliamentary Party of Charles Stewart Parnell and the Land League agitations of Michael Davitt attempted the former, while the Young Irelanders in the 1840s and the Fenians in the 1860s tried the latter course. Despite their different tactics, each served to make Britain's presence in Ireland more alien and the Irish more ungovernable. The one British political figure who stands out during this period was the Grand Old Man himself, William Ewart Gladstone. As the historian D. G. Boyce put it: 'Gladstone believed that, in the case of Ireland at least, politics had a destination, and the Irish question a solution.'

His efforts at delivering Home Rule for Ireland dominated late Victorian and Edwardian British politics. 'My mission is to pacify Ireland,' he proclaimed at the 1868 general election. Gladstone began by disestablishing the Church of Ireland, which served to underscore the decline of the old Protestant ascendancy. In 1873, the Home Rule League was formed to campaign for a restoration of the Irish Parliament, managing to win more than half of the seats in Ireland (aided, no doubt, by this being the first general election to employ the secret ballot). The next few years were dominated by the question of land reform with poor tenant farmers mobilised under the National Land League, founded by Michael Davitt and headed by the MP Charles Stewart Parnell. The Land League demanded reform of the rotten system whereby absentee landlords could charge extortionate rents and evict tenants on a whim. In one memorable incident, the league's direct action included refusing to harvest the crop of Lord Erne, an absentee landlord, whose agent, a Captain Charles Boycott, subsequently entered the lexicon as a verb.

In 1885, Parnell's Irish Parliamentary Party found itself holding the balance of power in Westminster. The following year, Gladstone brought forward the first of three Home Rule Bills, which was nevertheless defeated at its second reading. 'Home Rule Means Rome Rule' was the cry of opponents (although Parnell, like so many Irish Nationalists before him, was in fact a Protestant). Following Parnell's death in 1891, the octogenarian Gladstone brought forward a second Home Rule Bill in 1893. This time it passed its Commons stages but foundered in the Conservative-dominated House of Lords.

The first two decades of the twentieth century brought further tumult. In 1905, Sinn Féin was formed to campaign more vigorously for Irish separatism, while at Westminster, the Irish Parliamentary Party, now under the leadership of John Redmond, pursued the constitutional route. Following the two general elections in 1910, the Irish once again held the balance of power and used the advantage to press Herbert Asquith's Liberals to bring forth a third Home Rule Bill. With the Parliament Act in place, establishing the primacy of the House of Commons over the House of Lords, the prospect of achieving Home Rule was at last in sight. In the north of Ireland, Edward Carson, a Dublin Protestant barrister, led opposition to it. At this stage, there was no desire to divide the 'Protestant north' from the 'Catholic south'. However, Unionist opposition became increasingly militant, with the formation of the Ulster Volunteer Force (UVF) to forcibly resist Home Rule, if necessary. Conservative leader of the opposition Andrew Bonar Law told a rally in Belfast: 'I can imagine no length of resistance to which Ulster can go in which I should not be prepared to support them.' To underline their opposition, Unionists established a petition, 'Ulster's Solemn League and Covenant'. So intense was the feeling that some were said to have signed in their own blood.

By September 1914, the third Home Rule Bill passed its parliamentary stages but was suspended by the outbreak of the First World War. Carson urged the UVF to enlist en masse and they formed the 36th Ulster Division, going on to take heavy casualties at the Battle of the Somme. Redmond similarly urged the Irish to join up to fight for 'the rights of small nations' in the expectation that Home Rule would be delivered. Sensing the British had yet again welched on a deal, Irish Republicans saw a chance to drive a preoccupied Britain out of Ireland for good. The Easter Rising of 1916 is, more than any other, the seminal moment in twentieth-century Irish history. An armed insurrection, centred on Dublin, saw rebels take control of strategic buildings and sites across the capital and battle British forces for a week until being forced to surrender. The subsequent treatment of the leaders – courts martial and firing squads for sixteen of them – outraged Irish opinion. The days of British rule in Ireland were numbered.

In 1919, those Irish MPs who had been elected in the previous year's general election refused to sit in Westminster and formed a breakaway parliament, Dáil Éireann, to act as a rallying point for the country. A guerrilla war against British rule in Ireland began, with the government despatching mercenaries to supplement the police and army. Their mismatched uniforms earned them the sobriquet 'Black and Tans' and their notorious barbarity against the civilian population simply hardened the resolve of the Irish against British rule. In Dublin, the director of intelligence of the nascent Irish Republican Army, Michael Collins, wiped out a network of British intelligence agents, assassinating them simultaneously one Sunday morning. The same day, at a Gaelic football match in Dublin's Croke Park, British soldiers, ostensibly preparing to search men leaving the ground, opened fire on the crowd, killing fourteen people including two boys aged ten and eleven. The events of 21 November 1920 became known as 'Bloody Sunday'. (Again, Irish history repeats itself and there would be another, even more notorious, Bloody Sunday to come.) In 1922, a treaty was negotiated that would see an Irish Free State established, under the British Empire, while six counties of the historical province of Ulster would split off to form Northern Ireland. The treaty was narrowly supported in the Dáil, although it couldn't stop civil war breaking out in Ireland between those for and against it. Eventually, Irish Free State forces prevailed. The treaty was implemented, and Northern Ireland went its own way.

The years between partition in 1922 and the suspension of Stormont in 1972 were characterised by the growth of deep inequalities between Catholics and the numerically superior Protestants of Northern Ireland. The province's first Prime Minister, James Craig, infamously described Northern Ireland as 'a Protestant Parliament and a Protestant State'. The basic premise was that if Catholics didn't like how things were run, they could go and live in the south. The sectarianism was palpable. In 1934, the Unionist Minister of Agriculture (and subsequent Prime Minister), Sir Basil Brooke, was explicit in urging employers 'not to employ Roman Catholics, who were 99 per cent disloyal'. His Minister of Labour colleague, J. M. Andrews, was pleased to respond to a rumour that twenty-eight of the thirty-one porters at

Stormont were Roman Catholics: 'I have investigated the matter, and I find that there are thirty Protestants, and only one Roman Catholic there temporarily.'

These attitudes permeated every corner of the state. Electoral boundaries were gerrymandered to ensure Unionist hegemony wherever possible. This was significant because Northern Ireland was a patchwork of small local authorities. By the late 1960s, there were some seventy-three local authorities for a population of just 1.5 million. Crucially, the franchise for local elections was on the basis of property ownership, not universal suffrage. It was estimated that in 1961 over a quarter of the parliamentary electorate were disfranchised at local elections. Moreover, the retention of company votes entitled business directors to more than one ballot paper. This allowed housing allocations to be rigged and municipal jobs to go to the 'right' people. Discrimination was built into the fabric of Northern Ireland. It was state-sponsored, all-pervasive and seen to be a reasonable course, channelling generations of ingrained hostility towards Catholics from the Reformation onwards. Meanwhile, the Ulster Special Constabulary, the so-called B-Specials, were on hand as a quasi-militaristic, sectarian police force that would achieve notoriety for their brutal baton-wielding at civil rights demonstrations.

The former IRA hunger striker turned playwright Laurence McKeown described his first experience of discrimination when, as a young boy in the 1960s, his father applied to the local council for planning permission to build a bungalow. He was sure the plan would be approved because he borrowed a plan that a Protestant colleague of his had previously used successfully. Yet McKeown's father's application was rejected by his local council on no fewer than thirty-nine grounds. 'It was the first time I saw my father take a stand,' McKeown recounted in an interview with the *Irish Times*. 'He got a lawyer and appealed. The lawyer pointed out the council had passed the exact same plans a couple of years previously. Suddenly all the objections disappeared apart from three face-saving ones. It was only in later years that I realised it was to do with civil rights.'

But even buttoned-up Northern Ireland was not immune from the swinging '60s and the country found itself pulsating to a modernising beat. A Unionist moderate, Terence O'Neill, became Prime Minister of Northern Ireland in 1963. Captain O'Neill was a moderniser, keen to transcend Unionist and Nationalist identities which had become 'a ludicrous anachronism' that he wanted to replace with 'normal twentieth-century politics based on a division between left and right'. Alas, his good intentions did not inoculate him from the occasional bout of foot-in-mouth disease. Despite believing it made sense to treat the Catholic minority decently, his explanation for doing so was not particularly elegant:

> It is frightfully hard to explain to Protestants that if you give Roman Catholics a good job and a good house they will live like Protestants because they will see neighbours with cars and television sets; they will refuse to have eighteen children. But if a Roman Catholic is jobless, and lives in the most ghastly hovel, he will rear eighteen children on National Assistance. If you treat Roman Catholics with due consideration and kindness, they will live like Protestants in spite of the authoritative nature of their Church...[2]

However, change was in the air. President Kennedy paid a state visit to Ireland in 1963 and the IRA's border campaign (which mainly consisted of blowing up electricity substations along the border) had petered out the previous year. The time was ripe for a change of direction. Northern Ireland had ossified long enough. At Westminster, Labour leader Harold Wilson was on the cusp of a landmark general election victory over the jaded Tories, by now led by former hereditary peer Alec Douglas-Home, a kindly 'One Nation' grandee who did his sums on an abacus. The omens looked to be in favour of change.

However, not to labour the point, Northern Ireland is not Britain. A gust of fetid air has a habit of blowing in through an open window, confounding those arrogant enough to believe that history only moves in a linear direction. Faced with Unionist intransigence and growing calls for civil rights from the Catholic minority, O'Neill quickly found himself overwhelmed. In Belfast, Catholics were coming in for regular attack by Loyalist gangs intent on burning them out of their homes. By 1969, events were spiralling out of control. Harold Wilson's Labour government sent troops to Northern Ireland to support the Stormont administration in restoring public order. Initially welcomed by Catholics, fearing Loyalist mobs, the mood quickly soured, and they became seen as an occupying army.

The hostility shown to the civil rights movement started to harden into more urgent demands for equality. Specifically, the protesters were drawing attention to the policy of internment without trial, introduced in August 1971 to round up supposed IRA members. Out-of-date information and unreliable sources meant it was a spectacular disaster. Three hundred and forty-two people were initially arrested and taken to makeshift camps – all of them Catholics or Republicans. Over the next forty-eight hours, twenty-four people were killed, eleven of them by the British Army in the Ballymurphy area of Belfast, including a Catholic priest and a mother of eight.

Outrage over internment saw more protests and confrontation. This culminated on 30 January 1972 in a march for civil rights in Derry. Although the authorities had banned it (a tactic that had previously frustrated Daniel O'Connell's efforts), it went ahead anyway. The particulars of what happened next are one of the more familiar tales for British audiences. Soldiers from the Parachute Regiment opened fire on marchers, shooting dead thirteen people; a fourteenth subsequently died of his injuries. Here was another 'Bloody Sunday'. The presence of journalists and television cameras meant the world was given a front-row seat from which to witness Northern Ireland's carnage. This was the final straw.

Eight weeks later, fifty years of devolved government at Stormont came to an end and the Parliament was prorogued; the inevitable conclusion to a sorry tale of misrule and incompetence which had blackened Britain's name around the world. Not only was Northern Ireland completely out of control but the political class in Stormont was a fundamental part of the problem. If civil functions could not be discharged equitably, then Whitehall would have to run the place. After boarding the aeroplane at the end of his first visit to Northern Ireland in 1970, Home Secretary Reginald Maudling remarked to his staff: 'For God's sake, bring me a large scotch. What a bloody awful country!'

*   *   *

There is a wall in the Northern Ireland Office with photographs of the various Secretaries of State in chronological order. It's a mosaic that tells the story of the British government's uneven efforts in dealing with Northern Ireland after the imposition of direct rule in March 1972 right the way through to the completion of the Good Friday Agreement and the succeeding years when the process was embedded. It starts with that urbane old fixer Willie Whitelaw. He took over as Stormont was being mothballed. His tenure was best remembered for a short-lived ceasefire and talks where leaders of the Provisional IRA were invited over to London for discussions. The delegation included a young activist from Belfast and a former butcher's apprentice from Derry. It is quite a thought that Gerry Adams and Martin McGuinness (for it was they) were at the top table of Northern

Ireland negotiations for the next forty years. Throughout the mayhem of the mid-1970s there were faltering efforts at dialogue and another brief ceasefire. But the instability and violence of the times meant that political efforts quickly foundered.

During the 1970s and 1980s, the figures that followed were often stern-looking types with military bearing. Men like Humphrey Atkins, Tom King and Patrick Mayhew fitted the part perfectly. Occasionally, someone more imaginative was appointed, like Jim Prior or Peter Brooke, but there was little political buy-in at the time to progress the dialogue they sought. The Kremlinology is instructive. From the 1970s to the 1990s, the Northern Ireland brief was a political backwater, with ministers expected to remain wedded to the grim status quo that Northern Ireland simply needed a sufficiently robust security response to bring it into line. Indeed, British government policy towards Northern Ireland from the early 1970s to the late 1980s met Albert Einstein's classic definition of insanity: repeatedly doing the same thing and expecting a different result each time. This approach summed up Roy Mason's tenure. He was appointed Northern Ireland Secretary by Labour Prime Minister James Callaghan, serving between 1976 and 1979, and the legacy of this period is a grim litany of repressive measures and a casual disregard for legal due process and human rights. This was the era of the 'dirty war', when pretty much anything went. Torture of terrorist suspects, deployment of the SAS, jury-less trials and even the miasma of state agencies colluding with Loyalist paramilitaries – all were sanctioned as part of the war against the Provisional IRA.

Northern Ireland had been an international PR disaster for the British government since the late 1960s and under Mason there was a concerted attempt to 'normalise' the situation. This meant the Royal Ulster Constabulary (RUC) and Ulster Defence Regiment (the largest infantry in the British Army and, effectively, a local militia) assumed greater frontline roles in managing security. That both institutions were almost exclusively Protestant – the RUC was 90 per cent, the Ulster Defence Regiment 98 per cent – and merely locked in a 'them and us' mentality for the Catholic–Nationalist minority was lost on Mason.

But his other legacy – the 'criminalisation' of paramilitary prisoners (denying them political status and treating them as ordinary criminals) – had even bigger repercussions. Republicans started by refusing to wear prison uniforms, wrapping themselves in prison blankets instead. This escalated into a 'dirty protest', whereby they refused to 'slop out', instead spreading excrement over the walls in their cells. Yet Mason and his securocrat agenda were unbending. It is a demonstration of how hard-line his approach became that Margaret Thatcher continued it, leading, as it inexorably would, to the hunger strikes in 1981, in which ten Republican prisoners starved to death in protest. The propaganda victory became a potent recruiting sergeant for the Provisionals. Violence simply begot further violence and on it continued right through the 1980s and 1990s.

Eventually, however, politics broke through. In 1989, Peter Brooke, an aristocratic 'One Nation' Tory, succeeded Douglas Hurd at the Northern Ireland Office. In a carefully crafted phrase, Brooke asserted that Britain had no 'selfish strategic or economic interest' in Northern Ireland and would accept unification if there was majority consent. 'It is not the aspiration to a sovereign, united Ireland against which we set our face, but its violent expression,' he added.

This approach, coupled with secret talks between John Hume, leader of the constitutional-Nationalist Social Democratic and Labour Party (SDLP), and Sinn Féin president Gerry Adams, created the space for politics to take root and to eventually end the Provisional IRA's campaign and bring Republicans in from the cold. To be sure, it was a process that came in fits and starts, but the public recognition from the British government that it had no long-term special interest in Northern Ireland remaining part of the British state was a powerful symbol that an elegant withdrawal, at a time unspecified somewhere down the road, was possible.

Events picked up pace during John Major's premiership, with an eventual IRA ceasefire in 1994 and the publication of a series of concordats with the Irish government that would later pave the way for the Good Friday Agreement in 1998. However, things started badly. In 1991, the IRA launched an audacious bid to wipe out the British Cabinet. A van-mounted mortar was fired at Downing Street from across Whitehall. As the head of the explosives section of the Anti-Terrorist Branch, who defused one of the unexploded shells, explained in a (perhaps unintendedly) candid assessment:

It was a remarkably good aim if you consider that the bomb was fired 250 yards [across Whitehall] with no direct line of sight. Technically, it was quite brilliant and I'm sure that many army crews, if given a similar task, would be very pleased to drop a bomb that close.[3]

Although significant political breakthroughs came on Major's watch, he was reliant on Ulster Unionists in the House

WHY WE ARE WHERE WE ARE

of Commons to shore up his minority government, which had lost a string of by-elections as it imploded over Europe and the post-Thatcher agenda. After 1997, though, there was a shift in tempo. Enter Tony Blair. As Prime Minister, he and a succession of talented ministers took huge strides in building a political process that cemented the tentative peace accord. The line-up on the wall in the Northern Ireland Office became a 'who's who' of many of New Labour's brightest stars: Mo Mowlam, Peter Mandelson, John Reid, Peter Hain and (my old boss) Shaun Woodward.

Blair, the arch-pragmatist, whose governing credo was 'what matters is what works', recognised the potential for a transformational breakthrough. He appointed Mowlam as the first-ever female Northern Ireland Secretary. An earthy former academic anthropologist, she had been suffering from a brain tumour and as a result of her treatment had taken to wearing a wig. It is said she unnerved Unionists with her habits of removing it in meetings and calling everyone 'babe'.

The space opened up by the Good Friday Agreement meant the watchtowers and razor wire could be pulled down. The soldiers disappeared from street corners and returned home. In a landmark review of policing, the former chairman of the Conservative Party Chris Patten recommended the Royal Ulster Constabulary should be rebuilt from the ground up as the more neutral-sounding 'Police Service of Northern Ireland', with targets to recruit a representative number of Catholics. Mason's 'criminals' were released on licence in their hundreds (a critical move to facilitate progress, and one it is hard to imagine a Conservative government making). Blair's political adroitness represented the victory of dialogue and persuasion over the brainless, unflinching militarism that had gone before. Of all the things Blair did or did not do in his decade as Prime Minister, the Northern Ireland peace and political process is one of the unsullied entries on his scorecard. 'The peace process' is the familiar shorthand for what was, in essence, two processes – yes, a peace process, where the gun could be removed from Northern Irish politics, but also a political process, whereby Northern Ireland's tribes could be encouraged to come together in a power-sharing administration and, hopefully, focus on more everyday concerns. The two are, even to this day, symbiotic. The promise of reconciling political objectives through exclusively peaceful methods holds the 'men of violence' in check, while the absence of conflict allows long-held material grievances to be addressed. Is it perfect? No. But politics is famously the art of the possible, not the perfect.

This, then, is a flavour of the weight of context for understanding why we are where we are in relation to Northern Ireland. British historical narrative doesn't really know how to include Ireland, so tries not to. This brief canter through 800 years of British/English–Irish relations may seem unfamiliar. It probably jars, feels remote and doesn't fit with Britain's view of itself, then or now. It's a frustrating legacy for contemporary ministers who are sent to make sense of Northern Ireland and its complex backstory. Reginald Maudling's exasperation speaks for every minister who followed in his footsteps. However, the point of drawing attention to these events from Ireland's past is that they reverberate in the modern age. They help explain Irish suspicions about the trustworthiness of British statesmen, or Protestant worries about being sold out by the English. For most of us, they just pose awkward questions. Why would we raise a statue outside Parliament to a mass murderer like Cromwell? Why would we stand by and allow more than a million Irish to starve to death when their lands produced an abundance of food? Why would we send mercenaries like the 'Black and Tans' to kill and terrorise what were, in essence, British subjects? Why would we ignore the sectarianism of Unionist rule in Northern Ireland for fifty years? Why would we not instinctively side with the civil rights movement in the late 1960s, before we sent in the troops and allowed British soldiers to shoot fourteen protesters dead on Bloody Sunday? Why? Why? Why?

CHAPTER TWO

BRITAIN'S JUST NOT THAT INTO NORTHERN IRELAND

In many respects, the hardest question to answer in relation to Northern Ireland is also the simplest. Why is it still part of the United Kingdom? It is one of British politics' great puzzlements. A century-old sticking plaster that was applied to avoid a messy and violent ethno-national conflagration on the island of Ireland in the first two decades of the twentieth century has endured for, seemingly, no other reason than political inertia. Certainly not because the dispensation created at the time of partition was a success. In fact, the creation of Northern Ireland is one of the worst decisions taken by any British government during the whole of the twentieth century (and certainly one of the most expensive), leading, as it did, first to the creation of a sectarian state that abused the position of a third of the population for half a century before eventually metastasising into what euphemistically became known as 'the Troubles' and an incalculable loss of life and treasure up until recent times.

The endurance of Northern Ireland as an appendage to the United Kingdom ('of Great Britain *and* Northern Ireland') owes much to its marginal proximity. A province of just 1.9 million people (an equivalent population to the sleepy southern English county of Hampshire), it is in no meaningful way part of the UK at all. Geographical reality sees to that, with the torrents of the Irish Sea providing a permanent physical barrier from Britain. (Even at its narrowest point, from Belfast to Stranraer, the distance is around twenty miles – equivalent to that between Dover and Calais.)

It is, to an English audience, a faraway place of which they know and perhaps care little. To be sure, the Scots, kissing cousins of Northern Ireland's original 'planter' Unionists (those lowland Scots Protestants sent to Ireland in the Cromwell era to create a loyal garrison population), may retain lingering affections for their brethren; but that sentiment no longer courses through the bloodstream of the vastly more populous English – if, indeed, it ever did. And given emigration patterns from Ireland into the west of Scotland from the time of the famine, even Scotland is a house divided on the question of Ireland (with a quarter of the population having Irish ancestry). Writing here in England, Northern Ireland is seen as a strange little place, full of odd and violent people with whom the English have next to no affinity. Befuddlement, irritation and despair are more common emotions. We wonder why the IRA used to want to blow us up and why men in orange sashes and bowler hats want to march down streets where they are not welcome. If we think of them at all.

Northern Ireland is our unloved lodger. We are forced to cohabit because of some binding agreement signed by our forefathers from which there is seemingly no pain-free escape clause. However, the nature of our relationship is contractual rather than emotional; a dubious inheritance from a beleaguered interwar government facing the reality of making a messy concession in the face of a guerrilla war it could not win on one side and the emotional blackmail of Ulster Loyalists on the other. It chose what it believed was the lesser of two evils, unable to manufacture an elegant withdrawal from Britain's first colony. So, it split the difference, granting independence over most of the country to a Republican insurgency it could not suppress, while creating a protectorate for Loyalists it didn't love but felt it owed. For a state whose empire then covered a quarter of the globe, it was a large, humiliating concession. The Easter Rising of 1916, a week-long insurrection by armed Republicans against British rule, began a process of events which, over time, would signify the beginning of the end of the British Empire, with countless other national liberation movements taking their lead from Ireland's example. Hardly surprising, perhaps, that a succession of governments paid little attention to the vestigial statelet of Northern Ireland; a painful reminder of a national defeat.

In return, members of Northern Ireland's idiosyncratic political class were given carte blanche to run their affairs as they saw fit. In fact, the creation of Northern Ireland in 1921 was the most ambitious example of devolution ever allowed by the centralising twentieth-century British state. 'Metro mayors' may be the latest innovation in British politics, but for fifty years, Northern Ireland had its own Prime Minister. The crude majoritarianism built into the gerrymandered settlement was, however, an open invitation for Unionists to act corruptly. So, act corruptly they did, determinedly controlling the levers of power, removing political and economic agency from, as they regarded them, the numerically and religiously inferior Catholics. The spoils of the state were kept for the 'right' people: the 'loyal' Protestant–Unionist people.

There are innumerable books detailing the discrimination at the very heart of the Northern Irish state between the partition of Ireland in 1922 and the imposition of direct rule from Whitehall in 1972; suffice to say that these events are little discussed and poorly understood in British politics. Not helped by the fact that British MPs were forbidden from tabling parliamentary questions about Northern Ireland, as it was considered a devolved matter.

Britain joined the Irish in their tradition of linguistic understatement, referring to the events that took place from 1968 until the late 1990s as 'the Troubles' (just as the Second World War was referred to in Ireland as the 'Emergency'). We sought to minimise the horror of a secessionist uprising, with the fallout felt across many English cities and towns, reducing it to the status of 'a little local difficulty', like neighbours quarrelling over a privet hedge. A row that nevertheless saw the British Army's longest-ever campaign take place within the borders of its own country.

We should not be surprised at this particular type of British amnesia. When it comes to remembering our role in Irish affairs, there is much we would like to forget. When acclaimed British film director Ken Loach's Palme D'or-winning *The Wind That Shakes the Barley* was released in 2006, it played on 300 screens across France but just forty in the UK. The film depicts the activities of a 'flying column' of young IRA activists in County Cork during the War of Independence against British rule, focusing on the eventual split between pragmatists and purists over the treaty signed with Britain that paved the way for the creation of the Irish Free State but which also led to the partition of the country, fuelling the subsequent Civil War of 1922–23.

To the Irish, the key events and personalities of those tumultuous years have become second nature. Michael Collins. The Black and Tans. Éamon de Valera. The War of Independence. Partition. But to most people in Britain, all this represents a secret history. It is not taught in our schools or depicted on our televisions. In 2016, the Irish state broadcaster RTÉ commissioned a landmark period drama, *Rebellion*, on the centenary of the Easter Rising of 1916, yet it did not air on British terrestrial television, despite the events being just as much part of the warp and weft of British history. If, indeed, there is a single difference between the Irish and the English, it comes down to understanding why the Brits are always cast as villains in Hollywood blockbusters. The English are puzzled and a little bit hurt at the constant depiction of their countrymen as scoundrels and heartless murderers. On the receiving end of a litany of English misdeeds down the centuries, the Irish instinctively recognise why they are.

When Martin McGuinness first visited Downing Street to meet Prime Minister Tony Blair as a member of a Sinn Féin delegation, he was shown into the Cabinet Room and remarked: 'So this is where the damage was done.' Blair's chief of staff, Jonathan Powell, the man who oversaw the Northern Irish peace process for Blair, assumed McGuinness was referring to the 1991 IRA mortar attack on John Major's Cabinet. McGuinness had to explain he meant the signing of the treaty back in 1922 that divided the island of Ireland. If the foundational events of the Irish Free State are little understood by the English, the same applies to the Troubles. Again, memories of unwise and unjust political decisions mean there is little appetite for dwelling on the past. And there is much to forget. From the early 1970s and the imposition of direct rule, successive ministers sanctioned things that, fifty years on, are rather embarrassing to be associated with. In more recent times, since the peace process began, we are used to our Prime Ministers playing the part of the 'honest broker' rather than participant in the conflict, but this is a relatively new role.

British state papers released in December 2015 under the thirty-year rule revealed that in 1985 Margaret Thatcher suggested to her Irish counterpart, Garret FitzGerald, that the town of Dundalk, over the border in the Irish Republic, could be bombed in a bid to stymie fleeing Republicans who sought sanctuary there. The reports do not appear to capture FitzGerald's reaction to this suggestion of what amounted to state-sponsored terrorism, but Thatcher's mindset is instructive. It reflected the 'securocrat' belief that a military solution was possible against the Provisional IRA. This was, regrettably, the default British government view throughout the 1970s and 1980s. Former Labour Northern Ireland Secretary Roy Mason personified this dunderheaded machismo, remarking that he was going to squeeze the IRA 'like toothpaste' and bragging before Labour lost the 1979 election that the 'Provos' were 'weeks away' from defeat, despite the fact the Troubles were only at the halfway point.

Other state papers published in 2014 revealed a plan cooked up by the Northern Ireland Office to redraw the boundary, setting out a series of options which included ceding most of heavily Catholic Derry to the Irish Republic and, potentially, handing over West Belfast. This was to be achieved by turning it into a 'walled ghetto'. In a wonderful piece of understatement, the *Irish Independent* reported:

'Officials later noted that while moving half-a-million people – mostly Catholics – might be acceptable for a totalitarian regime, human rights arguments would be an obstacle.'

In a not-too-subtle bid to get unwanted Catholics out of a freshly carved Northern Ireland, it was suggested there could be loyalty tests in order to claim benefits, while 'large-scale' internment was also suggested as a means to help 'drive out large numbers'. Stories like this are easy to dismiss as eccentric kite-flying, but when they are remarks made by the Prime Minister of the country, or proposals drawn up by her officials and put before her, they are given a chilling validity. These crazy suggestions – and others which have not yet seen the light of day – reveal how extreme official thinking became. Indisputably, Margaret Thatcher had a jaundiced view of the Irish. Perhaps Peter Mandelson's vignette about meeting her soon after he was appointed Northern Ireland Secretary in 1999 sheds some light:

> She came up to me and she said, 'I've got one thing to say to you, my boy.' She said, 'You can't trust the Irish, they're all liars. Liars, and that's what you have to remember, so just don't forget it.'
>
> With that she waltzed off and that was my only personal exposure to her.[1]

In 2001, it came to light that Thatcher had suggested to a senior diplomat who was negotiating with the Irish government over the landmark Anglo-Irish Agreement in 1985 that Catholics living in Northern Ireland could be moved to live in southern Ireland instead. She made the suggestion to Sir David Goodall during a late-night conversation at Chequers. He explained:

> She said, 'If the northern [Catholic] population want to be in the south, well, why don't they move over there? After all, there was a big movement of population in Ireland, wasn't there?'
>
> Nobody could think what it was. So finally, I said, 'Are you talking about Cromwell, Prime Minister?' She said, 'That's right, Cromwell.'[2]

What shaped Thatcher's dislike of the Irish? Was it the loss of her close colleagues, MPs Airey Neave and Ian Gow, in Republican bombings, or her own near miss at the hands of the IRA in Brighton in 1984, when they detonated a bomb in the Grand Hotel during the Conservative Party conference? Or was it simply that a Grantham girl remembered Old Ironsides fondly? (Cromwell's first successful battle of the English Civil War was to capture the town from Crown forces.)

With so little regard for the Irish, it is perhaps no wonder that Britain's record during those dark years of the 1970s, 1980s and 1990s was a catalogue of controversial counter-insurgency measures that were first used to quell insurrections in places like Aden and Kenya, upheld by a belief that if you treat the natives firmly enough, they will eventually yield. There is much that to contemporary eyes is simply astonishing. Not to mention reeking of double standards. Indeed, if you think Guantánamo Bay, the infamous US detention centre for Islamist suspects in Cuba, has been an affront to legal due process, try internment without trial, introduced in Northern Ireland in August 1971 with hundreds of innocent men (all of them Catholics or Republicans) dragged from their homes and incarcerated without charge. Think the notorious Abu Ghraib prison in Iraq, where prisoners were systematically mistreated by Western forces, was appalling? Clearly you have never heard of Castlereagh detention centre and the torture programme carried out behind its walls by agents of the British state on what were, when all was said and done, British citizens.[3]

Then there's the 'hooded men' case of 1971, where fourteen ordinary Catholic men were rounded up during internment and subjected to 'deep interrogation' techniques, which included hooding, being forced into stress positions for long periods, being exposed to white noise and deprived of sleep, food and water. In 1978, the European Court of Human Rights judged their treatment was inhuman and degrading but stopped short of calling these infamous 'five techniques' torture. (The Bush administration later used that ruling as the legal basis for its own interrogation programme in Iraq and Afghanistan.)

The 'Ballymurphy Ten' were civilians gunned down by the British Army during the implementation of internment and a few months before the better-known 'Bloody Sunday' atrocity occurred. In both instances, soldiers from the Parachute Regiment were responsible, proving that few lessons were learned.

Think shoot-to-kill is rough justice when applied to jihadi terrorists with guns? It was also an approach used against the civilian Catholic population in Northern Ireland – not just the IRA (upon whom it was unquestionably used) – in the early 1970s as the army's shadowy Military Reaction Force ran amok.[4] These were plain-clothed soldiers operating, in the estimation of one of their number, as a 'death squad', shooting at indiscriminate targets from cars in drive-by killings, with no other purpose, it seems, than to induce terror. Conveniently, records of their activities have since been destroyed.

Not to overlook the really murky stuff.

Like the 'dirty war' counter-insurgency effort handled by the British Army's anodyne-sounding Force Research Unit, which ran agents and targeted Republicans for assassination, including Gerry Adams and Martin McGuinness.[5] This included figures such as Brian Nelson, who, while working as a British agent, was also a high-ranking member of the Loyalist Ulster Defence Association (UDA) and was personally implicated in twenty-six murders, including one of the most notorious – that of Catholic solicitor Patrick Finucane in 1989, who was shot at point-blank range fourteen times while his wife and children looked on in horror at the kitchen table of their Belfast home.

Then there was 'Agent Stakeknife' – alleged to be IRA hard man Freddie Scappaticci – the highest-ranking agent the British had in the Provisional IRA, who was responsible for their internal security unit, which interrogated, tortured and killed informers. It is suggested Scappaticci is responsible for dozens of killings, many of whom were presumably other British assets.

These are just some of the 'known knowns' in terms of what we definitely know was sanctioned by successive British governments against – let us not forget – their own people within the borders of the British state. Actions carried out in our name. These events are little understood on the British side of the Irish Sea, but if they had taken place on the streets of London, how would we react? Is it even remotely conceivable that police officers could round up people from English cities with no charge before subjecting them to 'deep interrogation'? How would we react if student protesters or vicars and pregnant women were killed in Trafalgar Square, or in the streets of Nottingham or Manchester, by our own soldiers?

Furthermore, it raises the question: if this is what we know happened, with no one seriously disputing that the above events took place in the ways described, just how bad are the 'known unknowns'? The events that took place during the Troubles that have still to come to light? Would some sort of truth and reconciliation process, of the kind frequently talked about in Northern Ireland in a bid to heal wounds and 'deal with the past', reveal, for instance, that British agents inside Republican paramilitaries deliberately targeted civilians in some of their infamous bombings to discredit them? After all, the level of British infiltration was such that it is claimed a quarter of Provisional IRA members were working for British state security agencies, rising to half of the organisation's senior management.

The point about collusion, whether in connection to

Patrick Finucane's assassination or in any of the dozens of other cases that we know about, is that it makes Britain culpable in state-sanctioned murder. It instantly reduces the state to a participant in the conflict, something successive governments have been loath to concede. It seeps into the grain of Britain's international reputation, leaving an indelible bloody mark. We tumble off the moral high ground and, in turn, partly validate the actions of Republican paramilitaries who, throughout the Troubles, always posited they were 'at war' with Britain. Collusion is a powerful leveller that reduces us to the status of a South American junta or an African dictatorship. Places where governments torture and murder their political opponents.

But collusion is not only about conspiracy to commit murder with proxy paramilitaries; it's also about creating a culture of impunity where the truth is actively covered up. This was brought to light by the Police Ombudsman for Northern Ireland's report into the 1994 Loughinisland massacre, where Loyalists opened fire in a crowded rural bar, killing six patrons and wounding five. The initial investigation into the murders was characterised by 'incompetence, indifference and neglect'.[6] Although the police knew the suspects' names within twenty-four hours of the shooting, they deliberately delayed making arrests. Nor did they investigate allegations that an RUC officer warned suspects that they were to be arrested – and that one initial suspect was in fact an RUC informant. The ombudsman, Dr Michael Maguire, found that police records had been destroyed. Is this evidence merely of police bungling? Or even just a case of overstretched officers punch-drunk from investigating the litany of killings during the Troubles? The ombudsman's assessment bears quoting:

> There has been considerable debate in academic publications, reports by non-governmental agencies and in the various inquiries into allegations of State-related killings in Northern Ireland. No consensus has emerged as to what it actually means ... I am of the view that individual examples of neglect, incompetence and/or investigative failure are not automatically evidence of collusion. However, a consistent pattern of investigative failures may be considered as evidence of collusion depending on the context and specifics of each case. This is particularly the case when dealing with police informants, who were participating in crime.[7]

In other words, 'collusion' is not just active participation with Loyalist paramilitaries but also the connivance to cover up the truth by, in this case, frustrating the investigation by warning suspects and destroying and tainting evidence. Summing up the catalogue of malfeasance by the RUC in 1994, the ombudsman said he had 'no hesitation' in determining that collusion is a significant feature of the Loughinisland murders.

Again, what right do we have to upbraid the world's less than savoury regimes for the treatment of their people, telling them to remove the mote from their eye, while we continue to have a plank sticking out of ours?

What was the view about collusion from within Whitehall? How did the conversations go? 'Minister, can we have clearance to defeat the Provisional IRA by siding with Loyalists and getting them to do our dirty work?' Perhaps it wasn't quite that stark. Given the civil service's love of euphemisms, did mandarins and securocrats talk about 'neutralising' their opponents? Or 'seeking a conclusive victory, using whatever methods are deemed sufficient'? There will certainly have been talk about not 'handing a propaganda victory' to the IRA by charging British soldiers, spies and officials who sanctioned, planned, implemented and covered up acts of collusion with paramilitaries. Perhaps the still-classified state papers of the 1970s and 1980s, which approved the dirty war against the IRA and then turned a blind eye to its inevitable consequences, capture more than bureaucratic indifference to this moral squalor. Hopefully, there were other voices in the discussion, pleading to stop and think of the consequences.

However, it's unlikely we will ever be given the chance to find out. There is little appetite for raking over the coals of Northern Ireland's bloody history from any of its parties, but there is none, whatsoever, from Whitehall. There is little to no prospect of an international body hearing former paramilitaries, soldiers, spies and officials state flatly what they knew or what they did during three decades of bloody internecine conflict. We will continue to hear talk of 'dealing with the past', but there will be no 'Oprah-fication' of Northern Ireland's Troubles, with all its messiness poured forth for the purposes of communal 'sharing'.

We want to forget about the place and overlook what we did there. The British government simply has too much to lose from the truth emerging, especially if it washes up at the doors of former ministers and politicians. Three thousand six hundred people were killed during the period and countless more were maimed, but there is little common ground about how and what is commemorated, remembered or conveniently forgotten. And, crucially, who is brought to book, either legally or in moral terms, for the deaths and atrocities that occurred. Of course, no one will publicly disown the idea of some sort of truth recovery process, but everyone has something unpleasant to answer for.

If Britain struggles to come to terms with the past, then it needs to be honest about the future. There is plainly no interest in remaining in Northern Ireland, whose place in the Union is attached by nothing more adhesive than convention these days. Discussions about Northern Ireland invariably see the chamber of the House of Commons empty. Not a single British newspaper saw fit to reflect on the fiftieth anniversary of the introduction of internment. Recounting the first time she met Boris Johnson, who was a senior colleague at the *Daily Telegraph*, the respected political commentator Rachel Sylvester recounted: 'He came into the newspaper's tiny office in the House of Commons, plonked himself down at the desk next to mine and declared that he was writing about Northern Ireland. "Remind me," he said, "which ones are the orange johnnies?"'[8]

Quizzed about whether he had ever read the Good Friday Agreement by former independent Unionist MP Sylvia Hermon, during a parliamentary committee exchange in 2019, former Brexit Secretary Dominic Raab replied testily: 'It's not like a novel where you sit down and you say, "Do you know what, over the holidays, this is a cracking read."'[9]

Perhaps the acme for the sheer intellectual lack of

interest that Westminster shows for Northern Irish affairs came in the first interview given by Theresa May's Northern Ireland Secretary Karen Bradley. The quality of Northern Ireland Secretaries certainly dipped from 2010 onwards. Bradley freely admitted that when she started the job she did not understand some of Northern Ireland's 'deep-seated and deep-rooted' issues. 'I didn't understand things like when elections are fought for example in Northern Ireland, people who are nationalists don't vote for unionist parties and vice-versa,' she said.[10]

Quite how a middle-aged, professional politician – a Cabinet minister, no less – someone who would have grown up with the Troubles as the backdrop of her daily media consumption during the 1980s and 1990s, could still be so oblivious to the fundamentals of Northern Ireland's idiosyncratic politics is bewildering. Or, then again, perhaps it is not. The corollary to not understanding even the elementary aspects is that most British politicians simply do not care. Would they, for instance, cancel their holidays to trudge the highways and byways of West Belfast or North Antrim, making the case for people there to remain part of the UK if a referendum on its constitutional status ever came to pass? Aside from a few dewy-eyed Unionist ultras, my guess is they wouldn't fill one half of a single Ryanair flight.

This was not the case when Scotland was on the table. Campaigners from all sides of British politics were happy to do whatever was needed to avert a Scottish breakaway. There were historical and emotional connections that were thought to be worth preserving, not least the complex economic and administrative ties that bind Scotland to England. There is no similar affinity discernible in relation to Northern Ireland. And, given the province is reliant on British handouts to stay afloat, there is no negative economic impact to it leaving. Dealing with the aftermath of a vote to leave the UK and join the Irish Republic is a simple case of 'lifting and shifting' sovereignty, with no ill effects felt on the rest of Britain.

So why have successive governments not moved to do so? There was clearly reticence for a long time because of the terrible price paid by so many Northern Irish families during the Great War. The Loyalist blood spilled as the 36th Ulster Division was mown down at the Somme in 1916 was a potent, visceral reminder to British politicians of the sacrifice of the Unionists. The message was clear: Britain owed them a blood debt. But the First World War is now consigned to historical memory. Put bluntly, there is no one left alive in Northern Ireland who suffered the privations of the First World War who can yell 'traitor' with any moral purchase at backsliding British politicians. Moreover, our understanding of those years has now evolved, with far more appreciation now (rightly) paid to the tens of thousands of Catholics who fought in the British Army as well, on the basis that this would lead to a commitment to finally free Ireland from Britain's grasp.

We treat Northern Ireland as some other place because that's precisely how we regard it. Perhaps one single measure, more than anything else, summarises this. The use of baton rounds and water cannons to quell civil disturbances has become a regular feature of the policing and security response. Yet they remain unused in Britain. In fact, their use in any British city, or against, say, student demonstrators, would be utterly unthinkable. When he was Mayor of London, Boris Johnson rashly purchased two second-hand water cannons following the London riots of 2011, only to be publicly slapped down by then Home Secretary Theresa May, who flatly refused him licences to deploy them.

In most of the media coverage of the various disputes in Northern Ireland, their regular usage merits little more than a passing remark. In fact, they are invariably – and incorrectly – described as 'non-lethal'. However, the University of Ulster found that their use during the Troubles led to the deaths of seventeen people, nine of whom were aged eighteen or under. We have acquiesced when it comes to tolerating such barbaric practices because we regard Northern Ireland differently; a place where it is permissible to employ quasi-military tactics against civilians with a casualness that would have British MPs screaming at ministers if deployed anywhere else. That we have normalised these brutal practices against civilians, whatever their cause, within a corner of the British state, is an appalling, dehumanising relic.

The otherness with which Britain regards Northern Ireland is, in fact, long-established government policy, ever since Peter Brooke's 'no selfish strategic or economic interest' speech which repositioned Britain as an honest broker, rejecting territorial chauvinism and instead upholding 'the principle of consent'. This has been the position ever since. So long as the majority want to remain part of Britain, this wish will be honoured. Of course, this is hardly a ringing endorsement of the status quo. No one in British politics seems to care about making the case that Northern Ireland *should* remain part of the UK, as they are more than happy to do with Scotland or Wales.

Northern Ireland is in a category of its own. Indeed, nowhere else does Britain effectively share sovereignty with another state as it does with the Republic of Ireland over Northern Ireland, from the time of the Anglo-Irish Agreement back in 1985 onwards. There is no similar arrangement with the Spanish over Gibraltar, or with Argentina over the Falklands. The Good Friday Agreement effectively placed Northern Ireland in an antechamber. If there is a majority that opts for Irish unity at some stage, then change will take place. No one is making a first-principles argument for Northern Ireland to remain part of the UK come what may. Indeed, nowhere else in British politics are our political leaders so flexible when it comes to our territorial sovereignty. Where Scotland is seen to be an opportunity worth holding onto, Northern Ireland is quietly regarded as a problem eventually worth jettisoning.

Scottish and Welsh elites in politics, business and culture are deeply integrated into British public life. In contrast, Northern Ireland's political class find few soulmates in Westminster. Unionist politicians – famously more British than the British – are now oddities in our system. When former DUP First Minister Peter Robinson defended an evangelical Christian pastor, James McConnell, over the latter's description of Islam as a 'heathen' and 'satanic' religion in 2014, it is easy for Unionist politicians to seem like something from a different planet. Not to mention the double standard. If Robinson had been a minister, a frontbencher or leader of a council in Britain, and allied himself with such blatant Islamophobia, he would have been out on his ear.

Following the 2017 general election in which Theresa May's disastrous campaign frittered away the Conservatives' parliamentary majority, she was forced to cook up a 'confidence and supply' arrangement with the Democratic Unionists, described in a *Daily Mirror* headline as a 'coalition of crackpots'.[11] Such was the controversy, even in the Conservative Party, that May's Education Secretary, Justine Greening, and the popular then leader of the Scottish Conservatives, Ruth Davidson, publicly voiced their reservations about the deal because of the DUP's perceived homophobia.[12] (Hardly surprising when the DUP's former leader Ian Paisley ran a campaign called 'Save Ulster from Sodomy'.)

All of this reflects the essential fact that the British and Ulster Unionist sensibilities are firmly on different tracks. The only reason Northern Ireland's status is not more openly questioned is down to the sheer relief that the Troubles are over. Surely Unionists can see that one day this will not be enough. Although the Irish state renounced its territorial claims to Northern Ireland, previously written into its constitution and conceded as part of the Good Friday Agreement, the status of the north-easternmost six counties of Ireland will remain contested.

Yet it is democratic agitation, rather than armed struggle, that will continue to gnaw at the fraying ropes holding Northern Ireland in the Union. This is set in the context of British–Irish relations having steadily improved over recent decades. Indeed, in her state visit to Ireland back in 2011, Her Majesty laid a wreath to the IRA volunteers who fought against Britain in Ireland's War of Independence (to be sure, many had fought *for* Britain during the First World War). The prospect of 'Dublin rule' is no longer, plausibly, a spectre for Unionists. Not when even the Queen herself can pay her respects to dead IRA men and women.

Although British–Irish relations have been buffeted by the fallout from Brexit, and there may be future turbulence ahead, they are a peach compared to the situation in previous decades. Indeed, this growing amity provides a fulcrum upon which continued debate about the relationship between these isles can mature.

Things are changing in the north too. While the 'sectarian headcount' may be a crude measure of political allegiance, it is worth noting that Catholics now outnumber Protestants at every level of Northern Ireland's education system.

(Tellingly, this is true in the former Unionist citadels of Belfast and Derry.) Northern Ireland's in-built Protestant Unionist majority is shrinking; while the integrative logic of an all-Ireland offering to the outside world is increasingly important in terms of investment and tourism. In time, a similar referendum to the one we saw in Scotland will come to pass in Northern Ireland. When it does, it will be hard to imagine the British political class busting a gut to maintain the status quo.

Unionists need to accept this basic political reality and mentally and emotionally prepare themselves for its inevitable consequences. Although the Good Friday Agreement copper-fastens the principle of consent, they should read the small print. The other way of viewing this safeguard is that Northern Ireland is the only part of UK with a constitutional guarantee that a transfer of sovereignty *can* take place when the majority wishes it.

There are, then, two distinct political choices in the years ahead. The first sees us maintain the fiction that Britain wants to retain Northern Ireland and that this constitutional arrangement represents the settled, unflinching final will of the people. This view would, logically, see Northern Ireland more fulsomely subsumed into the British state. Yet integration is precisely what its political elite – Nationalist and Unionist alike – *doesn't* want. Clearly, Republicans and Nationalists hate the idea of having their identity diminished by becoming more British, but there are downsides for Unionists too. Westminster's decision to legislate for abortion rights in June 2019 has caused severe irritation for the DUP. With Catholic influence over the SDLP waning, Unionists find themselves deprived of one of the few cross-community issues where there was a shared moral outlook. Moreover, the peremptory way in which British MPs legislated for the rights – tacking it onto other legislation in the face of Unionist opposition – has left a bitter taste, with DUP ministers since refusing to implement the provisions.

While Nationalists want to develop sinews with the south in a bid to 'Irishise' the province, stretching from demands for Gaelic signage through to cross-border development bodies, Unionists simply want maximum local autonomy and freedom to manage their own affairs *sans* power-sharing with Catholic–Nationalists, if they could get away with it. They recognise their particular traditions – the Orange marches and instinctive social conservatism – are now seriously out of step with the British mainstream.

The second big choice, then, about Northern Ireland's future would see all parties – the British, the Northern Irish and the southern Irish – facing up to the glaring reality that partition of the island of Ireland is archaic. A historical compromise born of the fear of something worse that has simply lost its sting over recent years. Between 1921 and the collapse of Stormont in 1972, the default British position was one of complete indifference. After that, it was one of belligerence in the face of the Provisional IRA's campaign. Ministerial chest-puffing during this period crowded out any critical thinking about what was in the long-term best interests of the British people. (Ironically, the Provisional IRA's long campaign did much to prop up this intellectual *ancien régime*.) Now, with the situation transformed by twenty years of incremental political progress, there is little excuse for further inaction.

The stabilisation of politics within Northern Ireland will, in turn, serve to strengthen cooperation with the Irish Republic. The integrative forces – economic and demographic among them – will force a re-examination of its constitutional status. British politicians will be delighted if this occurs. Especially at the prospect of long-term savings. The £10 billion a year the British Exchequer pumps into Northern Ireland to plug its budget deficit – the gap between what it raises in taxes and what it spends – is equivalent to £27 million a day. If Northern Ireland was no longer on Britain's balance sheet it is unlikely that a decade's worth of austerity would have bitten as hard for the British people, and Boris Johnson's pledge to 'level up' public spending in the north of England would be a much easier task. An unfair comparison? Not when Northern Ireland is increasingly viewed as a quixotic choice and one, given the option, we may wish to change our mind about. Indeed, a 2019 poll of Conservative Party members showed a clear majority – 59 per cent – prioritised securing Brexit, even if it meant the disintegration of the UK and the loss of Northern Ireland.[13]

The simple truth is that a lack of imagination among the British political elite is the only thing now holding up the chain of events that will test Northern Ireland's constitutional status in a border poll. In the decade to come, a combination of economics, demographics and changes to the British state, particularly the impact of English devolution and the prospect of Scottish independence, as well as the continued liberalisation of southern Ireland, with the emergence of Sinn Féin as a party of government, will make Irish unity look like the inevitable, logical end point of the fractured, bloody history of these isles.

The question, then, for British politicians is simple: would it not be better to start preparing for that day?

CHAPTER THREE

SHEER MAGNETISM: HOW ECONOMIC INTEGRATION MAKES A SINGLE IRELAND INEVITABLE

At the time of writing, the Northern Ireland Protocol is operational. Despite the vehement opposition of Unionist politicians and Loyalist paramilitaries, the provision to avoid the imposition of a hard border on the island of Ireland by introducing post-Brexit customs checks on goods coming into Northern Ireland from Britain at the ports has resulted in a boom in trade between Northern and southern Ireland, with a corresponding fall in trade between Britain and Northern Ireland as the more stringent inspections on goods make it more onerous for smaller exporters to do business.

Unionists despair at this situation for three reasons. The

first is that the protocol results in a border in the Irish Sea and, as such, constitutes a philosophical affront to their sense of identity, making their Britishness more conditional and less secure. Second, as mentioned, the protocol makes exporting from Britain more burdensome, with extra checks and paperwork. Although there has been talk of empty shelves in Northern Ireland's shops as a direct consequence, this claim is hotly contested, with many pointing out that the province is less severely affected by the availability of consumer goods than the rest of the UK has been over the same period. What it certainly does mean, however, is that many Northern Ireland businesses have rerouted their supply chains into southern Ireland and simply got on with things.

Capitalism has little concern for identity politics, but this fillip for north–south economic cooperation is another affront for Unionists, creating, they contend, an 'economic united Ireland'. The third and perhaps more prosaic reason Unionists oppose the protocol concerns Loyalists, or more specifically the UDA and UVF paramilitary groups, which are still in operation, although they are primarily concerned these days with the importation of hard drugs into Northern Ireland. Part of the reason they are so aggrieved is that the rigorous border checks are making it more difficult to import cocaine and other Class A drugs from Britain, their main supply route.[1]

By the time you read this, events may have deteriorated. The Democratic Unionists are threatening to crash the devolved institutions unless the protocol is scrapped, and British ministers, led by Lord David Frost, the government's chief Brexit negotiator, are threatening to unilaterally activate Article 16 of the protocol, a break clause, which states:

> If the application of this Protocol leads to serious economic, societal or environmental difficulties that are liable to persist, or to diversion of trade, the Union or the United Kingdom may unilaterally take appropriate safeguard measures. Such safeguard measures shall be restricted with regard to their scope and duration to what is strictly necessary in order to remedy the situation. Priority shall be given to such measures as will least disturb the functioning of this Protocol.[2]

Unionists maintain the protocol has led to just such a scenario. As previously mentioned, the claim that Northern Ireland is in any way facing shortages on the shelves is moot; however, it is clear that trade is being diverted, but that is the very essence of a market economy. If I cannot purchase the goods that I need from supplier A at the price that I want to pay, then I will try my luck with supplier B. It is shouting into the wind to suggest otherwise. Unionists oppose greater inter-Irish trade for no other reason than they want to inhibit the growth of north–south economic development in principle. *Econo-sectarianism.*

Former Ulster Unionist leader Lord (Reg) Empey described as 'intolerable' the fact that British businesses were developing all-Ireland supply chains in response to the protocol. 'Many of us have long suspected that the intent of the EU all along was to recalibrate Northern Ireland's trade by closing off traditional supply routes with the rest of the UK and facilitating trade between NI and the EU,' he claimed in June 2021.[3] Empey also blamed the British government, stating that '[they] should never have proposed a border on the Irish Sea', as well as his hated rivals the DUP: '[They] should never have supported this anti-Unionist solution. We are all now paying the price for this blunder.'

The figures are stark: In the first six months following Britain's self-ejection from the EU, exports heading south–north were up by 40 per cent year on year and up 54 per cent since 2018, while figures for north–south trade grew by 61 per cent since 2020 and 111 per cent since 2018. The east–west trading route saw similarly dramatic effects.[4] Goods exports from Britain to Ireland fell by 32 per cent in the first half of 2021 (a drop of €2.9 billion compared to the first half of 2020). In contrast, exports of goods from Ireland to Great Britain jumped to €1.42 billion in June 2021 (an increase of 68 per cent, year on year).

There are certainly 'societal' problems stemming from the protocol – if that is shorthand for the outrage felt across Unionist politics – but the problem here is that Unionism is now a minority concern in Northern Ireland. No one apart from their dwindling cohort is affronted by the protocol or its contended effects. Moreover, it bears noting that Loyalist displays of anger throughout 2021, violent and sinister though they were, have been nowhere near the shows of strength that Ian Paisley mustered in opposition to the Anglo-Irish Agreement in the mid-1980s. Back then, he could get 100,000 people out on the streets. The best-attended protests over the protocol have scraped barely a couple of thousand demonstrators.

All of which led Dr Adam Posen, president of the respected Peterson Institute for International Economics and a former external member of the Bank of England's Monetary Policy Committee, to warn business leaders in Belfast in October 2021 that the border arrangements are unsustainable in the medium to long term.[5] 'Five to ten years down the road, we're looking at Irish unification because the economic forces at work just aren't going to be reconcilable with the political situation,' stated Posen. Although Northern Ireland's anomalous position – inside both the UK and EU markets – potentially brings huge advantages, to capitalise on this 'best of both worlds' scenario requires 'political maturity', Posen observed, which is evidently in short supply.

In any event, the focus of this chapter is on the economic case for Irish unity, and that starts with examining the underlying state of the Northern Irish economy. The broad thrust is this: Northern Ireland is an economic basket case. A century ago, it was an economic powerhouse. Belfast had the biggest shipbuilding industry in the world, creating the mighty *Titanic*, with a host of other industries in engineering and manufacturing, particularly linen production, also prospering. However, like other industrial centres in northern England, Northern Ireland underwent a precipitous decline in the post-war era. Like the mighty *Titanic*, industries like shipbuilding sank and thousands of secure, well-paid jobs went down with them. Almost imperceptibly, something else happened. Southern Ireland, for so long an economic backwater, hit its stride. A combination of low corporate taxes, a skilled and educated workforce and massive inward investment, much of it from the US, turbo-charged the Irish economy. Suddenly, the roles were reversed. Northern Ireland was the beggar, reliant on British handouts, while the 'Celtic Tiger' growled.

The later excesses of this period are well known, and Ireland certainly paid a price for the hubris of its greedy property speculators and lax politicians before recovering strongly in recent years, but Northern Ireland is still firmly in the doldrums, with a gaping fiscal deficit and high structural poverty and worklessness. The country is reliant on a £10 billion annual subvention from London to survive, with an engorged public sector and an anaemic private economy. As an illustration of the point, although it has a population of just 1.9 million people, the Northern Ireland Executive employs 23,000 civil servants, while the European Commission has 32,000 officials dealing with the affairs of the EU's 445 million population.

A report by the Northern Ireland Statistics and Research Agency (NISRA) on the 'Structure and Performance of the NI Economy 2016 and 2017' published in October 2021 highlighted how peripheral Northern Ireland's economy is to the UK.[6] The analysis compared the GDP of Northern Ireland, Scotland and the UK as a whole. It found that Northern Ireland's economy was worth £46.3 billion compared to £156.4 billion for Scotland and £2 trillion for the UK overall. Even accounting for the size differentials, this is marginal. Although Northern Ireland makes up 2.8 per cent of the UK's total population, it comprises just 2.2 per cent of its overall economy.

The UK's GDP per head was £31,326, while in Scotland it was £28,830 (92 per cent of the UK average), but it was just £24,750 in Northern Ireland (at 77 per cent of the UK average, it was nearly a quarter less). Unsurprisingly, Northern Ireland's labour market also lags behind UK averages in many key regards, with the lowest employment rate and the highest economic inactivity rate in the UK, according to NISRA figures for October 2021.[7] In 2017, 16 per cent of Northern Ireland's working-age population had no qualifications, twice the rate for the UK overall.[8] Deprivation and lack of social mobility (transcending the circumstances of one's birth) affect both communities in Northern Ireland, particularly in parts of Belfast and Derry, with many Catholic communities still grappling with ingrained poverty, while the educational attainment of Protestant boys from disadvantaged backgrounds trails every other group apart from those from Roma and Traveller communities.[9]

What higher-value employment there is relies heavily on the public sector, with the private sector having a preponderance of lower-productivity businesses – no doubt a legacy of Northern Ireland's troubled past as investors shied away. Changing these fundamentals remains a work in progress, with NISRA's latest 'Index of Services' from September 2021 showing output from the services sector was still 4.3 per cent lower than the highest point back in Q4 2006 when it first began measuring it.

There are two obvious conclusions to draw. The first is that Northern Ireland is the least valuable, dynamic and diverse part of the UK economy. Second, it is plain enough to see that the economic dividend of peace and political process has not been felt keenly enough. Clearly, thirty years of the Troubles hardly helped matters, but Northern Ireland's economic woes are deep-seated. Regardless of whether Irish unity is viewed as a panacea for Northern Ireland's problems, there has been remarkably little serious consideration about how the two parts of the island of Ireland could work together more harmoniously – improving their productive capacity and spreading prosperity – if they were part of a single state, with the strategies and assets of both parts of the island aligned and complementing each other for maximum effect. Theoretically, the benefits are clear: the border is an artificial division and the respective populations are small enough and complementary enough to make uniting their economic efforts a common-sense solution. Currently, it is as if Northern Ireland and the Republic are the only dinner guests positioned at opposite ends of a grand banqueting table.

Indeed, a major study published in November 2015 made the case that Irish unity brings with it massive economic wins for both parts of the island of Ireland.[10] 'Modeling Irish Unification' was the work of a respected team of academics led by Dr Kurt Hübner, director of the Institute for European Studies at the University of British Columbia. They modelled various scenarios, including the effects of fiscal harmonisation, the reduction of trade barriers, transportation costs and currency transactions, narrowing the productivity gap between Northern Ireland and the more productive south, the impact of joining the euro and the effects of fiscal transfers from the British state in plugging Northern Ireland's budgetary black hole. (Tellingly, it was the first such simulation of economic and political integration, which, given Northern Ireland's hotly disputed status, seems extraordinary.)

The results showed that 'political and economic unification of the north and south would likely result in a sizable boost in economic output and incomes in the north and a smaller boost in the ROI'. The report calculated that integrating the two jurisdictions could drive out value equivalent to €36 billion during the first eight years, and while the Republic would see a more modest, but still considerable, boost, the biggest effect would be to 'encourage foreign capital inflows into Northern Ireland'. The report argued that '"borders matter" to a much greater degree than most observers would expect'. And while both economies are interlinked and interdependent, they are not aligned, 'differ[ing] enormously in terms of structure, output and growth'.

The authors characterised the current differences between the south, which is 'a strongly outward-looking and export-intensive economy ... its long-term excellent growth record very much is based on a globally competitive regime of foreign direct investment', and the north, which is 'a relatively more inward-looking economy that shares features of an economic periphery inside the UK'. This results in gross value added (a measurement of sub-national economic growth) per capita being 159 per cent higher in the south and although both economies recovered from the 2008–09 global downturn, Northern Ireland still lags far behind. The Irish Republic's record in recent years – a highly competitive tax regime and a relentless focus on winning foreign direct investment – has 'earned the ROI the highest level of trade-openness among G20 nations'. Moreover, it is 'this kind of policy framework that can be anticipated in NI if it unifies with the ROI and becomes integrated into the island economy'.

The research team modelled a series of propositions in ascending order of optimism. They began by assuming that a unified Irish state picks up the costs of absorbing Northern Ireland from day one, but that adopting the Republic's tax regime and foreign investment policy platform has no immediate effect. Even in this pessimistic forecast, GDP across the island of Ireland would increase by €15.8 billion by 2025, a 3.1 per cent increase in GDP across the whole island. In their second assessment, they again assumed the Republic would pick up Northern Ireland's bill but that this time it did benefit from inward investment, accounting for all-Ireland growth of €31.2 billion by 2025. The least pessimistic assessment again sees the south inherit the north's debts while reducing duplicated public expenditure by 2 per cent a year, but this scenario realises the proper potential from foreign direct investment. This time, the accumulated gain for the newly integrated island of Ireland is €35.6 billion by 2025, with the benefits heavily weighted in Northern Ireland's favour by a 2:1 margin.

What the modelling shows is that the more thought-out and planned-through the scenario, the better the outcome.

This all may seem obvious, but there has been little in the way of serious analysis of the economic effects of Irish reunification and even less planning in that regard, and this report provided a serious benchmark for future work. It added much-needed empirical weight to intuitive common sense: both parts of the island of Ireland would be better off integrating their economic efforts for the benefit of all the people of the island of Ireland – assuming, of course, that the essential goal of any society is to improve the living standards of its people.

But this is Northern Ireland, and politics tends to get in the way. How do Unionists, wedded to a plainly failing status quo, answer the charge that Irish reunification makes economic good sense? Indeed, what the report shows is that hard-headed realism now belongs to those advocating a united Ireland, with Unionists reduced to denying reality and clinging to an outmoded, faith-based romanticism about the province's economic prospects. In 2018, Hübner and his team published a second report, again based on cutting-edge economic modelling. 'The Costs of Non-Unification: Brexit and the Unification of Ireland' set out a 'conservative case' for Irish unity as a response to Brexit, modelling three basic scenarios.[11] Writing before the British government's eventual withdrawal agreement, Hübner explored the effects of a 'hard' Brexit (the UK leaving the EU with no deal), a 'soft' Brexit (keeping Northern Ireland in the customs union and single market) and a third option of Irish unification. The relevant section of the report bears reproducing in full:

A hard Brexit would reduce the GDP of Northern Ireland over the period 2021 to 2025 by €10.1 billion. This represents a per capita loss of €5,035. In the scenario where Northern Ireland stays in the Single Market and the other parts of the UK opt for a hard Brexit, the accumulated loss of GDP would be smaller but still amounts to €3.8 billion. This reduction translates into a per capita loss of €1,921. The only winning scenario is the case of unification where between 2018 and 2025 NI would increase its GDP by €17.9 billion, i.e., an increase per capita of €9,070 over the period.

Of course, in the end, the British government went for the Goldilocks option: keeping Northern Ireland compliant with single market regulations under the aegis of the Northern Ireland Protocol. What both of Hübner's reports lay out in stark detail is that the rational option is to unify the two jurisdictions, certainly if the goal is to make best use of economic assets and increase GDP and living standards.

Partition and Brexit systematise low growth and low productivity and leave people in Northern Ireland worse off than they would otherwise be.

Currently, the annual subvention from the British Exchequer – covering the fiscal gap between what is raised in taxes and spent on the public sector – props up Northern Ireland's economy. Coming in at £10 billion a year, it underscores the sheer unreality of Northern Ireland's economy, and, as Hübner points out, unification would make it entirely unnecessary. For Unionist opponents of Irish unity, this fragility is a useful argument for maintaining the constitutional status quo. Could Dublin afford to take on the place? Would Irish voters want to potentially pay higher taxes to take back the 'fourth green field'? There have been attempts to deconstruct the subvention and unpick the real financial commitments. Professor John Doyle from the School of Law and Government in Dublin City University wrote a paper on the subject in June 2021 for the Royal Irish Academy in its journal, *Irish Studies in International Affairs*.[12] A third of the figure, £3.4 billion, is made up of pension liabilities, but current practice sees the British government pay out for pension commitments, even for non-UK residents if they have paid pension and national insurance contributions.

An additional £4 billion goes on UK national debt

contributions, military spending, other overseas costs and unspecified smaller items of spending. On Professor Doyle's calculations, the £10 billion figure can be whittled down by nearly three-quarters. In a piece for the *Irish Times*, he summarised his argument:

A subvention of €2.8 billion does not present a significant barrier to Irish unity and the economic debate on unity needs to move on to the more important questions of the policy decisions necessary to support sustainable economic growth to maximise the benefits of a larger and integrated all-island economy and to support improved public services in health, welfare, education and infrastructure. These will be the real issues that will shape the costs and benefits of a united Ireland and they will be central in the future referenda debates. Compared with those decisions the subvention is irrelevant.[13]

Irrelevant. Thus, southern fears of being lumbered with the north are unfounded. As are Unionist claims that the Republic cannot afford to take responsibility for Northern Ireland. The report makes clear that unity presents net benefits for both jurisdictions. This is before we factor in handover arrangements that would see, for example, Northern

Ireland once again being able to access EU regeneration aid and farming subsidies (which have been lost due to Brexit). It would also be likely that Britain would agree to a period of harmonisation during any transfer of sovereignty and make reasonable arrangements for any legacy commitments, such as pensions. After all, Ireland is one of the UK's main export markets and a successful integration of Northern and southern Ireland is in Britain's economic self-interest too.

One of the key aspects of economic integration between both jurisdictions is creating the same fiscal framework. Indeed, this has been surprisingly uncontentious in recent years, with the DUP even proposing the harmonisation of corporation tax levels with the Irish Republic. Former First Minister Peter Robinson, the leading proponent of the move, described winning permission from Whitehall to proceed with the plan as 'one of the achievements of the past few years that I am most proud of'.[14] It was a prize that came after a great deal of lobbying, with the last Labour government refusing the request (worried about increasing Northern Ireland's fiscal deficit with the UK Treasury) before David Cameron relented. The hope in Northern Ireland is that they will be better able to compete for foreign direct investment with the Irish Republic, which has enjoyed a corporation tax rate of just 12.5 per cent since 2003. (Although Ireland reluctantly agreed in October 2021 to a call from the Organisation for Economic Cooperation and Development to set a 15 per cent floor on corporate taxes.) Historically, Ireland has sought to make its economy more competitive through keeping business taxes low, much to the chagrin of other EU member states, who have criticised its aggressive fiscal regime, allowing it to cream off the spoils of international investment.

Yet with its lack of connectivity to the continent and dearth of mineral reserves, Ireland has simply made the most of what it has. In recent years, this has meant skipping over the Industrial Revolution and heading straight for the intellectual, capital-intensive industries of the knowledge economy. A young, well-educated workforce (nearly half the Republic's population – 49 per cent – is under thirty-five, whereas the EU average is just 40 per cent), a competitive tax regime, membership of the single market and a huge hinterland in the United States has provided a potent mix, with American companies accounting for two-thirds of foreign direct investment into Ireland.

The Celtic Tiger years, from the mid-1990s until the crash of 2008, saw the Irish economy soar, with growth rates of 5–6 per cent a year. In 2005, The Economist Intelligence

Unit found the Republic had the highest quality of life in the world, according to the basket of criteria in its quality-of-life index, beating Switzerland into second place (while Great Britain only managed the twenty-ninth spot). The boom – long, keenly felt and unprecedented in the history of the Irish state – was, as all debt-fuelled property booms are, built on quicksand. The fall, when it came in 2008, was precipitous and painful. As *The Economist* put it: 'Output from peak to trough fell by 21 per cent in nominal terms and unemployment rose from 5 per cent to 15 per cent. As house prices plummeted by 47 per cent, the banks collapsed and had to be rescued, which pushed the debt-to-GDP ratio to 123 per cent.'[15]

In 2010, the Irish government accepted (under duress) an €85 billion bailout programme from the European Central Bank, the European Commission and the International Monetary Fund. The Troika's 'assistance for austerity' terms forced the Irish government into three years of painful retrenchment to recapitalise its banks and rebalance its public finances. In December 2013, Ireland exited the bailout programme, becoming the first of the financially distressed Eurozone members to do so (and in the process, a poster boy for euro-austerity).

Fine Gael Taoiseach Enda Kenny, who inherited the deal

upon winning the 2011 general election and made many of the savage cuts required, delivered a televised address to the country to confirm Ireland was ending the programme early. He said that Ireland's 'good name' had been restored and that its future direction would be based on 'enterprise, not on greed', while the banking system would have to become a 'contributor rather than a huge drain [on the economy]'. Meanwhile, his Finance Minister, Michael Noonan, said that ordinary Irish citizens were the 'real heroes and heroines' of the story, describing the financial crisis as the worst Ireland had faced since the famine. Indeed, they were. As the Irish economist Paul Sweeney put it, Ireland lost 'almost a decade of economic progress'.

So, although Ireland went through the equivalent of an extreme boot camp to deal with its debt and banking problems, many of its other economic and financial fundamentals remained in robust health. In May 2016, the Institute for Management Development World Competitiveness Center (IMDWCC), a think tank measuring nations' relative economic competitiveness, reported Ireland moving from sixteenth position out of sixty-one advanced nations in 2015 to seventh position in 2016 (the UK was eighteenth). In its assessment of sub-categories, the IMDWCC found Ireland was first for 'Real GDP growth', 'Flexibility and adaptability of people', 'Real GDP growth per capita', 'Investment incentives', 'National culture' and 'Finance skills'. As clean bills of health go, it was as emphatic as it gets.

A key ingredient in this success has been the Republic's record of wooing foreign direct investment. The approach became a cornerstone during the Celtic Tiger years, but the strategy can be traced to the liberalising economic reforms of Taoiseach Seán Lemass in the 1960s. Although it was Henry Ford who was one of the first major foreign investors in the country back in 1917 when he opened a car plant in Cork, the birthplace of his father. It is said that by 1930, 7,000 of the 80,000 inhabitants of the city worked for Ford Motors.

IDA Ireland, the country's inward investment agency, continues this tradition. Its client companies have created in the region of 250,000 jobs, accounting for 12 per cent of all Irish employment, while the value of their exports is some €124.5 billion in goods and services and they pay €2.8 billion a year in corporation tax to the Irish state.[16] After a brief hiatus in 2008–09, when foreign investment was hit, a familiar pattern quickly resumed. (Although foreign direct investment fell from 23.9 per cent of Irish GDP in 2009 to 10.5 per cent in 2011, it rebounded to 19.4 per cent in 2012, and during the period 2009–12, despite its problems, Ireland was still among the world's ten biggest recipients of foreign direct investment as a proportion of GDP.)

As the Hübner research argues, attracting foreign direct investment is not only about a competitive tax regime but also, 'and in many ways more importantly, about restructuring an entire policy framework to attract and feed high value-added enterprises'.[17] What is particularly noteworthy is that the keenest proponents of lowering Northern Ireland's corporation tax rate are Democratic Unionist ministers. They adopt this approach as the most business-friendly of Northern Ireland's parties, but the irony of seeking fiscal harmonisation with a neighbouring state they affect to have nothing to do with seems lost on them. This blind spot is, though, down to the entirely commendable urge to take greater control of Northern Ireland's destiny. In his 2012 conference speech to the Democratic Unionist Party, then First Minister Peter Robinson lamented that before the Troubles began 'over 90 per cent of all expenditure by the Northern Ireland government was met by money raised here. And that should be our goal again.'[18] Fiscal autonomy was his objective, he explained, stating that the country should be 'not reliant on the central Exchequer, but an engine of economic prosperity in our own right'. Robinson and his successors are surely right to argue for such sensible measures, but do they, as Unionists, realise the political ramifications of harmonising tax rates between two such small jurisdictions? Such integrative logic only ever travels in one direction.

Yet it is perhaps further proof that economics will overtake Northern Ireland's stalled politics and deliver a form of economic unity before we see its political equivalent catch up. The original dichotomy between an industrialised, urban north, pitted against an agrarian, pre-industrial south has been spectacularly reversed in recent decades. In one key respect, the cities of Belfast and Derry are akin to many British cities and towns in that they have undergone structural economic decline, spurred on by the demise of traditional sectors and their replacement with lower-value, more insecure service industry work.

Meanwhile, the command-and-control economics of partition and the Troubles – all military spending and insurance underwriting of terrorist attacks – is now giving way to a more fluid arrangement, whereby the logic of a single, integrated offering in areas like tourism and attracting inward investment – as well as harmonising tax rates – are now mainstream positions to advocate. Capitalism is succeeding where politics has failed in modernising and redefining the relationship between the Irish and British states. Dispassionate, hard-nosed commerce will gradually develop a single Irish economy, whether the politicians drive the agenda or not. This, in turn, renders the border meaningless. Indeed, the various cross-border quangos established under the Good Friday Agreement to foster joint working are slowly seeing to that. Their very bureaucratic utility is a mark not of how portentous unity is, but how banal. Again, it is small, incremental steps that will see Irish unity become a reality.

After all, a state, like a human body, is held together by its constituent parts – bone, flesh and a central nervous system – each playing a role in the overall design. So it is with an economy, with trade routes, investment and shared infrastructure each contributing to a bigger whole. (Like the 86-mile, £200 million north–south electricity grid interconnector project that stretches across the border, linking together power grids across the island of Ireland.) Formal cross-border cooperation is also happening under the aegis of the North–South Ministerial Council, one of the bodies established by the Good Friday Agreement. Already, there are a series of arm's-length bodies in agriculture, environment, education, tourism, strategic transport and health planning administering chunks of public administration on a whole-Ireland basis. Rather than have this happen in a piecemeal, uncoordinated manner, it is surely better to shape these emerging trends to maximise their impact. Indeed, it is irresponsible not to have the political and economic directions of these two small, interconnected jurisdictions properly aligned.

After all, why should the hard-pressed British taxpayer continue to shell out £10 billion or so a year in a direct transfer that sees Northern Ireland remain one of the highest-subsidised parts of the UK? For every pound spent in the UK per head of population, £1.24 is spent per person in Northern Ireland (it's only 97p in England). Indeed, if devolving economic levers and a bottom-up, what-matters-is-what-works approach is the order of the day, there is only one logical direction of travel for Northern Ireland: closer joint working with the south.

The business community is already leading the way, with Chambers Ireland and the Northern Ireland Chamber of Commerce having established a 'formal affiliation' with each other in July 2016. Welcoming the move, Ann McGregor, chief executive of the Northern Ireland Chamber of Commerce and Industry, said: 'By affiliating with each other our two organisations will provide a stronger platform and greater opportunities for interaction for all businesses on the island of Ireland.'[19] Again, commerce is leading where politics is not.

Yet despite its many structural problems, Northern Ireland has, in estate-agent parlance, the potential to be 'an up-and-coming area'. But, to mix metaphors, Ireland wouldn't be Ireland without rain clouds looming on the horizon. The potentially game-changing issue for Northern Ireland that will compel hard economics to prod the province's indolent politics forward is Britain's decision to leave the European Union. In March 2016, three months ahead of the referendum, Northern Ireland's Department of Enterprise, Trade and Investment calculated the potential costs of Brexit, commissioning Oxford Economics to model a number of scenarios around the economic impacts of the UK leaving the EU. For the UK, it estimated a net economic loss in the range from 0.1 per cent to 3.8 per cent of GDP depending on the scenario. For Northern Ireland, the impact was more severe, with losses of up to 5.6 per cent of GDP.[20] In short, if Britain catches a cold by leaving the EU, Northern Ireland will get the flu. Even more galling given there was a clear majority (55.8 per cent) of Northern Ireland voters in favour of remaining in the EU. Indeed, Northern Ireland was one of only three regions/nations in the UK that did vote to remain

(Scotland and London being the others). In fact, the Foyle constituency in Derry recorded one of the strongest remain votes across the UK, with 78.3 per cent support for staying in the EU.

In the aftermath of the Brexit vote in June 2016, *The Guardian* interviewed a series of businesspeople in Newry, near the border with the Irish Republic.[21] Declan McChesney is the third generation of his family to run Cahill Brothers women's shoe shop in Newry. 'Personally speaking, I am on the floor over this Brexit vote,' he said.

> About 30 per cent of my business in this shop comes from the south and I am worried that if there is a crisis between the pound and the euro, will our products be too expensive for my southern customers? We have survived as a family business two world wars, the aftermath of the Easter Rising and the modern Troubles. Now we have a new crisis that never needed to happen here after all that we survived. It is deeply depressing.

This vignette underscores the 'real world' problems that business in Northern Ireland will face because of Britain's exit from the European Union. How will the resolve of the Unionist-led executive fare when presented with a loss of

EU funding, agricultural subsidies and regeneration cash, as well as the economic shock of leaving the EU and a flight of capital to the Irish Republic, where single market access is guaranteed? The challenges are significant but were flagged up in good time ahead of the Brexit referendum. Another report, this time by the devolved assembly's enterprise committee in March 2015, found that quitting the EU would cost Northern Ireland £1 billion a year – equivalent to a 3 per cent fall in economic output.[22] The report's author, Dr Leslie Budd from the Open University, argued that as well as damaging Northern Ireland's attractiveness as an entry route into the single market, transaction costs for trading into the EU would 'rise significantly' and inhibit economic cooperation with the neighbouring Irish Republic. Leaving the EU would also cut off vital funding that has done so much to copper-fasten peace in recent years. Between 2007 and 2013, Northern Ireland received £2.4 billion from the EU and continued funding deals up to 2020 were 'central to Northern Ireland['s] economic and innovation strategies'.[23]

The obvious question is *cui bono*? As the adage has it, England's difficulty is Ireland's advantage. The Industrial Development Agency Ireland's homepage sums up the difference between pro-EU Ireland and Brexit Britain perfectly:

Ireland is a committed member of the European Union and provides companies with guaranteed access to the European market. Ireland is the only English-speaking country in the Eurozone and provides an ideal hub for organisations seeking a European base. The brightest talent from across Europe is attracted here, mixing with our own to offer a multinational and multilingual melting pot of skills with a positive attitude to match.[24]

Subtle it is not. It is even more unnerving given that Northern Ireland's record on securing foreign direct investment is much shakier than the Republic's. Figures from the Office for National Statistics for sub-national foreign direct investment performance across the UK show that between 2015 and 2019 the value of Northern Ireland's stock declined from £19.2 billion in 2015 to £14.8 billion in 2019.[25]

* * *

What are we to conclude from all this? Perhaps most obviously, that the economics of Irish unity stack up. It is an affordable and entirely positive move, and, as the Hübner research shows, there is a 2:1 benefit for Northern Ireland joining with the south, putting wind into the sails of a newly integrated economy. In pure public finance terms, Britain loses an unproductive long-term asset from its balance sheet, freeing up investment that can be diverted to the English regions to make good Boris Johnson's rhetoric about 'levelling up' the British economy. Meanwhile, Dublin, which is increasingly reliant on inward migration, gains in terms of scale and domestic market.

So, the challenge is now laid down: why not realise the economic potential of a united Ireland? What is holding us back? It is time for politics to be as rational as economics. With Brexit posing very real risks to Northern Ireland's future prosperity, not least with the loss of EU funding and ongoing rows about the protocol, there is no time to delay. Irish economic unity represents a pragmatic, evidence-based alternative model from the current, discredited, supplicant system where a manifestly unsustainable Northern Ireland economy swims against tides that will surely one day overwhelm it. Usefully, Hübner's research also concludes there is 'no established order' between economic and political unification taking place. He pointed out that in the example of German reunification, economic harmonisation came before political union. This means, logically, pressing ahead with fiscal convergence, something Unionists were strongly in favour of a few years ago, but also developing stronger north–south ties around inward investment and infrastructure and accelerating cross-border cooperation.

For Britain, grappling with post-Brexit headwinds, as the Johnson government tries to reset its economic policy by investing in the north of England in the hope of retaining the swathe of 'red wall' seats it won from Labour in 2019, maintaining the economic deadweight cost of Northern Ireland becomes less and less attractive, to this government and to future ones. A resentful English electorate, which increasingly eyes the public spending settlements in Northern Ireland and Scotland jealously, will simply not countenance the current arrangements indefinitely. Not when English devolution presents us with a cadre of powerful provincial metro mayors fighting for their share of the national economic cake. It would seem supremely unlikely they will allow the debate about the iniquities of the Barnett formula – which sees a quarter more spent, per head, on Northern Ireland – to continue to be a closed discussion. Ultimately, for British politicians, there are no votes in Northern Ireland, and its bespoke problems will simply not command the same attention in the future as they have in the recent past.

So, what does a 'unity offer' or a 'unity dowry' look like? There are four key elements. The first is that the British contribution to the success of Irish unity should see sufficient funding put in place to secure the economic harmonisation that is necessary for the new Irish state to realise its potential. Realistically, Britain has a medium-term commitment of five to seven years before tapering off. This still represents fantastic value for the British taxpayer as a long-term commitment is taken off the books. As a key ally and export market Britain has an enduring stake in this transition working.

Second, this should be supplemented by the creation of an all-Ireland infrastructure fund. Public investment in Northern Ireland's infrastructure has long lagged behind that of the rest of the UK, so much so that Northern Ireland has among the highest smartphone usage in the UK because superfast broadband coverage is non-existent in whole parts of the province.[26] Annual capital investment in Northern Ireland runs at around £4 billion. Again, this is about half the figure for the UK per head of population (£2,173 for Northern Ireland, compared to £4,292 for the UK as a whole). In contrast, the Irish Republic has invested heavily in its basic infrastructure over recent decades. (Last year it completed a ten-year €34 billion national transport investment programme.) It also has ambitious plans to develop a renewable energy portfolio and has one of the most advanced and competitive telecommunications infrastructures in Europe.

Third, the new Irish state should move quickly to realise savings from the de-duplication of public functions, freeing up money that can be immediately reinvested. The Hübner research put this at 2 per cent of GDP in immediately achievable savings. Fourth, the integration of Northern Ireland and the Irish Republic secures membership of the European Union and access to the single market as well as EU aid and grant arrangements. This would help reverse some of the disruption generated by Brexit.

The economics of Irish reunification are compelling. A plan to bring it about is eminently achievable. The timing is apposite. The benefits would be felt widely across the island of Ireland. The question is not 'whether' the economics of Irish unity work; they do. The outstanding issue is encouraging the politics to catch up.

CHAPTER FOUR

BUYER COLLECTS: THE SOUTHERN APPETITE FOR UNITY

The implicit proposition of this book is that the Republic of Ireland has a desire to accept the six counties of Northern Ireland as part of its state. That there is, in the parlance of eBay, a willingness for the buyer to collect. It needs to be said at the outset that this is a major assumption and deserves careful interrogation. When asked in opinion polls how they view the prospect of reunification, there are voices among the Irish electorate that are strongly supportive; there are also those who see it as too abstract a question to merit much critical thought and some respondents who sense taking on the place is more trouble than it's worth. Some southern Irish people display an instinctive kinship with their northern brethren, while others see them as actually foreign.

There was a telling episode during the official Easter 1916 centenary commemorations when the great-great-granddaughter of the socialist revolutionary and signatory of Ireland's Declaration of Independence, James Connolly, was upbraided for not being Irish enough by an irate man in the invited audience: 'I was told I was being disrespectful towards 1916 for talking through a song, that the event wasn't about me, that I didn't belong there with an accent like mine and that I should go home,' 29-year-old Sarah Connolly complained. 'He repeated [that] I should go home multiple times.'[1] The irony, of course, is that Connolly himself was in fact born in Edinburgh and served seven years in the British Army.

A similarly insular, 26-county parochialism was on display during the 2011 Irish presidential election campaign. During a television debate, one of the candidates, Sinn Féin's Martin McGuinness, was assailed by a young woman in the audience, thus:

As a young Irish person, I am curious as to why you have come down here to this country, with all your baggage, your history, your controversy? And how do you feel you can represent me, as a young Irish person, who knows nothing of the Troubles and who doesn't want [to] know anything about it?[2]

Through the lens of British politics, it is possible to misconstrue the mood of the Irish Republic towards reunification of the country and assume there is alacrity among political elites and public to simply absorb the north. It's nowhere near as straightforward as that because the mood of the Irish people is far from straightforward, nor, arguably, has it ever been. Despite the fulsome commemorations for the centenary of the Easter Rising in 2016, it is often overlooked that the original events of that week were not always greeted with a surge of public support. Tales abound of how apprehended Volunteers were marched through the streets of Dublin to the jeers and scorn from passers-by angry at the destruction of their city.

Yet by the general election of 1918, Sinn Féin won three-quarters of the parliamentary seats in Ireland. Evidence, perhaps, that the Irish suffer from cognitive dissonance – holding two mutually exclusive opinions – in relation to how their freedom from Britain came about. A case of public respectability and private radicalism? Many – indeed most – Irish people would like to see the country reunified but blanch at the methods that have, hitherto, been employed to bring it about. While the prim and law-abiding Irish disown violence and criminality, the gun, as they say, has never been far from the ballot box. A cursory glance at the antecedents of Ireland's political class bears this out.

Although Sinn Féin is the oldest political party on the island of Ireland, formed in 1905, and the Labour Party (formed by James Connolly) is of a similar vintage, it is Fianna Fáil and Fine Gael that have proven the most electorally potent. Hard to categorise in left/right terms – and even difficult for British audiences to pronounce – both are Nationalist, centre-right and support free enterprise. Fianna Fáil, the more socially conservative of the two, is Christian democratic in nature, with stronger roots in rural Ireland. As it has shown governing Ireland for the past decade, Fine Gael is more pro-market and closer in temperament to an Irish version of the modern British Conservative Party.

In terms of their position vis-à-vis the question of Irish unity, both parties have impeccable Republican roots, reflecting the split in Irish politics between pro- and anti-treaty factions in 1922. Michael Collins, mastermind of the IRA's guerrilla war against the British, led the 'pro' faction that went on to become Fine Gael, while Éamon de Valera, a veteran commander of the 1916 Easter Rising, led the 'antis' and went on to form Fianna Fáil. In terms of their impact on Irish politics, it is the latter that has governed longest and left the biggest mark on Irish public life and society. Roughly translating from Gaelic as 'Soldiers of Destiny', Fianna Fáil remains an avowedly Republican party. The first aim of its eight-point constitution makes this clear: 'To secure in peace and agreement the unity of Ireland and its people.' The party's website explains that 'Republican here stands both for the unity of the island and a commitment to the historic principles of European Republican philosophy, namely liberty, equality and fraternity'.

Founded in 1926 by de Valera during a schism in Sinn Féin about whether to officially recognise the new Irish Free State and stand for elections, the fledgling party had, by 1932, formed its first government and moved to scrap the oath of allegiance to the British monarch that had been a requirement of the 1922 treaty. In 1937, the Irish electorate supported de Valera's proposed constitution – Bunreacht na hÉireann – which, inter alia, included a territorial claim over the six counties of Northern Ireland. Protectionism and populism were hallmarks of his approach to politics, and de Valera was not averse to tweaking the nose of the British for popular effect. He withheld land annuities from Britain, stoking a tit-for-tat trade dispute with Britain until it was resolved in 1938 in an agreement that gave Ireland jurisdiction over three 'treaty ports' that Britain had retained in southern Ireland since the foundation of the Free State (later allowing Ireland to remain neutral during the Second World War).

Fianna Fáil governed Ireland for most of the 1940s and 1950s, introducing key elements of the Irish welfare state, before de Valera bowed out as party leader in 1959 to be replaced by his protégé, Seán Lemass, a founding member of the party and, like de Valera, a veteran of the 1916 Rising. The pragmatic Lemass is credited with opening up Ireland's economy in the 1960s, offering grants and tax concessions to attract inward investment, bolstering Irish industry and setting the country on the road to joining the European Economic Community. It was a radical change of direction from the parochialism of the early de Valera era, with its narrow interpretation of national sovereignty.

Lemass also sought to normalise relations with Northern Ireland's new Prime Minister, Terence O'Neill, an initiative that looked promising until the events of the late 1960s spiralled out of control. By 1966, Lemass had passed the baton to Jack Lynch, who provided a steadying influence in subsequent years as the Troubles erupted. During the Battle of the Bogside in August 1969, as rioting engulfed the besieged

Catholics of Derry, Lynch went on state television and, in a remarkable address, called for the United Nations to intervene, and put the Irish Army on standby along the border, urging the British government to begin serious talks about Irish unity.

In trying to understand Fianna Fáil's political centre of gravity, it's worth viewing it as more of a Peronist movement. A national, rather than simply a conservative, party. (Indeed, the indefatigable de Valera went on to become President of Ireland, a role he held from 1959 to 1973, dying two years later, aged ninety-two.) Patrician, populist, pragmatic and used to governing, the party has been in power for more than twice as long as Fine Gael. It professes to represent 'the mainstream of Irish life' and, in a jarring piece of management speak on its website, claims to have a 'can-do attitude' with the aim of 'unit[ing] all in a common identity of self-confident Irish men and women in a dynamic, vibrant, prosperous nation'.

The party boasts that its electoral success down the years makes it 'second only to the Social Democrats in Sweden in its length of tenure in office'. As 'the single most coherent force in Irish politics', other parties in Irish politics 'have been characterised by their opposition to Fianna Fáil as their only common bond'. Modesty, it is safe to say, is not a trait the Soldiers of Destiny appear to have in abundance. Yet it is this brashness, this ability to engorge whole tracts of political space, that has seen them withstand any move to embed more familiar right/left politics in Ireland.

Indeed, Fianna Fáil's emblematic support for Irish unity has, hitherto, degraded Sinn Féin's appeal in the south (made easier by the Republicans' decision to ignore the validity of the southern state until 1986). In recent years, however, Fianna Fáil has suffered a reversal of fortune. Widely blamed for the excesses of the Celtic Tiger years, when Ireland's economy enjoyed double-digit growth before crashing, which led to swingeing austerity measures being imposed by the European Union and the International Monetary Fund, Fianna Fáil's political star has waned, and they have been eclipsed over the past decade and a half by arch-rivals Fine Gael and even ended up backing them in a 'confidence and supply' arrangement between 2016 and 2020.

Hopeful of breaking their losing streak ahead of the 2020 general election, Fianna Fáil's manifesto promised measures to improve relations with Britain following the bruising Brexit negotiations and to establish a 'Shared Island Unit' as part of the Taoiseach's office, focused on practical measures to foster north–south cooperation.[3] In a tetchy section entitled 'Work[ing] towards a consensus on Unity', the manifesto upbraided Sinn Féin (without mentioning them), claiming that constitutional change 'cannot be allowed to become a party-dominated issue, exploited for short-term reasons'. The unity of hearts and minds 'cannot be achieved in an aggressive, partisan manner'. Instead, the focus should be around 'a neutral and factual discussion of the impact of various approaches to Northern Ireland's future'.

A cautious man by inclination, Micheál Martin has been criticised by many in his party for leaving the field clear for Sinn Féin to own the issue of Irish unity, having repeatedly ruled out any movement on the issue over the lifetime of the current Irish government. One of his senior Teachtaí Dála (TDs, members of the Irish Parliament), and a potential successor as leader, Jim O'Callaghan, published a paper in March 2021 calling for detailed discussions to begin about holding a border poll, which, he argued, was likely 'at some stage over the coming decade'. He also sketched out a series of changes that would be required to accommodate the north in a new, single Irish state, going as far as suggesting Ireland's second chamber, Seanad Éireann, could be moved to Stormont in Belfast and that every Irish government might include Unionist representation. Such bold thinking highlights how seriously the next generation of Dublin's political leaders are starting to take the issue.

What of their chief rivals? Fine Gael represent the yang to Fianna Fáil's yin. Less successful electorally than their old rivals, the party's periods in office have been fewer and farther between. More economically conservative and less populist than Fianna Fáil, their 2020 manifesto claimed that 'personal liberty' is one of their key principles because individuals and families 'know how best to organise their own lives and make decisions for themselves'.[4] Traditionally, they are also more circumspect on the question of national unity, yet they still describe themselves in their manifesto as 'the United Ireland Party' and claim to be working towards the 'aspiration' of national unity 'based on the principle of consent and a clear majority, North and South, being in favour'. The operative words here being *clear majority*, a deliberately opaque reference which suggests a simple 50 per cent +1 result in a border poll would not be enough of a qualification (contrary, it is worth pointing out, to the provisions in the Good Friday Agreement). Again, like Fianna Fáil, their language is about a 'shared Ireland', which encompasses 'all identities, religions and minorities'. Their manifesto included the particularly trite phrase that uniting people 'is even more important than uniting territory'. In a parallel with Jim O'Callaghan's intervention, the Fine Gael TD Neale Richmond made another considered intervention into the reunification debate, writing a paper in April 2021 calling for a new, united Ireland to be 'respectful, warm and demonstrate genuine equality of opportunity' for Unionists, suggesting that Ireland should apply to rejoin the Commonwealth (it was a member until 1949) and that the national anthem and flag could change as a gesture that Unionist identity will be valued.[5]

While genuflecting before the issue of Irish unity, Fianna Fáil and Fine Gael both avoid taking firm positions or suggesting any practical steps to bring it about. (O'Callaghan and Richmond are outriders, in that respect.) A cynic might point out that this has suited the Irish, who are free to maintain their emotional connection with the idea of national reunification without having to worry about it ever happening. It is a particularly Irish sort of hypocrisy. To outwardly back unity has long been regarded as too radical and risked validating the tactics of 'the men of violence', something southern voters have always been loath to do. Yet the same cause remains unfinished business to the very same voters, hence they have traditionally been content to vote for Fianna Fáil.

In this respect, Dublin has been just as willing as Westminster to kick the reunification can down the road. Indeed, for all their claims to be a Republican party, Fianna

Fáil governments have often been eye-wateringly brutal in their treatment of Irish Republicans from the time of the Civil War right the way through the Troubles. It is still significant, however, that Irish political elites feel the need to pay homage to the issue of national reunification, and to commit to playing an active part in the affairs of Northern Ireland. The future of 'the north' maintains a spectral presence in Irish public life, with newspapers actively hostile to notions of unification, like the *Irish Independent*, reporting on it incessantly. It is for ever unfinished business.

Interpreting Irish public opinion vis-à-vis the reunification of the country therefore becomes an inexact science. It would be much clearer if it were to be discussed openly and rationally. What if the prospect of unification was wrested from Republicans and became a mainstream position, embraced by all quarters of the Irish political class who could get on with discussing the practical steps necessary to bring it about? We are already in what I would characterise as a period of 'post-Union, pre-unity'. Northern Ireland, as a concept, has never looked weaker. Take any issue you like. Brexit. Population changes in the north. Election results. Scottish independence. Each of them is game-changing and inches Northern Ireland towards the United Kingdom's exit door. The risk of inaction, of letting events simply take their course, is that Dublin eventually finds itself overtaken by them. The promise – the guarantee – of a border poll hinges on there being sufficient support in Northern Ireland. Belfast sets the pace and Dublin does not have a veto. It is wise, then, to keep in alignment and to understand that Irish unity is not some nebulous pipe dream; it is a process affecting both parts of the island of Ireland and the tempo will only quicken in the years to come. Dublin's politicians need to be participants not spectators and 'de-Shinnerise' the discussion, as both Jim O'Callaghan and Neale Richmond, through their thoughtful interventions, suggest.

All of which raises the question: where is southern Irish public opinion today in relation to the question of Irish unity? The first thing to note is that in Irish politics opinion polls are less frequent, making the development of the public mood harder to gauge. A good place to start, however, is an exit poll (so, actual voters) from the pollsters Red C for the 2019 European elections, commissioned by broadcasters RTÉ and TG4.[6] Voters were asked the following question: 'If there was a referendum on a United Ireland tomorrow, would you vote yes in favour of a United Ireland, or no against a United Ireland?'

Nearly two-thirds (65 per cent) answered in the affirmative. Fewer than a fifth (19 per cent) said 'no/against' and another 15 per cent said 'don't know' or refused to answer. When those undecided groups are excluded from the sample, the figures are even starker, with 77 per cent backing unity and just 23 per cent opposed. 3:1. Pretty dramatic top-line figures, but what is interesting are the detailed findings.

For instance, 68 per cent of southerners aged 18–34 were in favour of Irish unity. What is perhaps surprising is that this high level of support remains consistent throughout the age groups. It dips for the 35–44 age cohort, to 60 per cent (still conclusive, however) but lifts again to 66 per cent for every age group after that, including over-65s, who often tend to be the most conservative on 'change' issues. This indicates a deep level of support across the age groups, highlighting that, unlike Brexit in Britain, the issue of Irish unity doesn't divide southern voters on age. This makes it likely that the overall trend – strong support – is unlikely to waver over coming years.

Perhaps the group in southern Irish society that might be thought to be the least welcoming of major constitutional change is the professional middle class. Yet the figure for those from the 'ABC1' social grouping (professionals/senior managers) shows 60 per cent supported unity and just 22 per cent opposed it – again, a clear 3:1 margin. Support gets stronger 'lower' down the social strata – the point being that the poorer and more marginalised you are, the more strongly you back Irish unity, with support in category 'F' (semi-skilled manual workers) rising to 78 per cent. The classlessness of the appeal feels highly significant and, like the consistent support across the age demographic, it is evidence that support for Irish unity is widespread.

The biggest variation in Irish public opinion for unity comes down to geography. There's stronger support in rural Ireland at 70 per cent, dipping to 62 per cent in urban settings. Take the variation between voters in Dublin – 55 per cent of whom supported unity – and the people of Munster (in the south-west of the country) – where the figure is 70 per cent. In the rest of Leinster outside the capital, support rose to 67 per cent, while in the westernmost province of Connaught and the three southern counties of Ulster, it was at 68 per cent. Perhaps tellingly, the 'don't know/won't say' figure is highest in Dublin, at 22 per cent. Could this be accounted for by higher levels of inward migration to the capital? Do these age-old constitutional questions confuse newcomers? Given Ireland's high rate of immigration in recent years, might there be a lukewarm reaction to Irish unity from these groups when the referendum eventually comes?

Given that Fine Gael leader Leo Varadkar has shown little interest in the issue, he might be surprised to learn that support for Irish unity among his party's voters is at 66 per cent – second only to Sinn Féin's (85 per cent) – while just 22 per cent of Fine Gael voters were opposed. In contrast, the figures for Fianna Fáil are 65 per cent and 24 per cent respectively. Of all the main Irish parties, the Greens are the least, well, *green*. Just 54 per cent of respondents who vote for the party back unity, with a fifth (21 per cent) opposing it and just over a quarter (26 per cent) who don't know/won't say.

The remarkable thing here is that in all sorts of categories – age, class, geography, gender and political allegiance – there is strong, granular support for Irish unity. It's an issue that does not appear to divide southern voters in a significant way, with no real constituency of opinion opposed to the idea. Structurally, it would appear the issue is in rude health and there is an enormous amount for campaigners to build on.

Of course, the usual health warnings apply with any opinion poll. All pollsters stress that their work is a mere snapshot of opinion at a moment in time. The only constant is that people are wont to change their minds. On non-immediate issues that have yet to properly crystallise in the public's mind, responses can be general. Like British attitudes towards our membership of the European Union, which were positive only a short time before Brexit. There is something unreal about the public's responses until the issue to be decided looms into view as a real and imminent choice to be made. When voters are presented with theoretical options, they cannot be blamed for responding theoretically. If the 2014 Scottish independence referendum was anything to go by, once the poll was in prospect and the issues widely discussed, support for independence grew and, while not winning, the result – 55 per cent against independence, 45 per cent for it – was much closer than anyone in Westminster had anticipated. As Gerry Adams pointed out when making a post-Brexit comparison: 'It used to be in Scotland that it was men in kilts with big beards that wanted independence, and then it became a real-life issue.'

Campaigns count for a huge amount and serve to catalyse opinion and polling numbers shift as a result. As no one is engaged yet on a sustained basis with the question of whether there should be Irish unity, we should approach any findings with a degree of caution. Indeed, it is worth pointing out that another poll from 2015, commissioned by the BBC and RTÉ, showed that although there is strong basic support for the proposition that the country should be reunited, southern voters blanched at the prospect of paying more taxes to bring it about. The 66 per cent of voters who backed a united Ireland in their lifetime increased to a commanding 73 per cent if it meant paying less tax – but more than halved to 31 per cent if it meant paying more.[7]

*　　*　　*

Following the February 2020 general election, Irish politics has a new buyer that is extremely willing to take on the north. The old Fianna Fáil/Fine Gael duopoly is in decline following a dramatic surge by Sinn Féin, winning the popular vote on a 10.7 per cent swing, and just being pipped from returning the highest number of TDs by a single seat (Fianna Fáil won thirty-eight seats to Sinn Féin's thirty-seven in the 160-member Dáil). The party's failure to stand a full slate of candidates in the expectation of making only modest advances in the Republic's single-transferable-vote system limited their breakthrough.

Nevertheless, it was still a watershed result, making Irish politics a three-horse race. So long the outsiders, and easy for the established parties to demonise as the political wing of the IRA, the Shinners played a masterful game, focusing on big-ticket domestic concerns, particularly around the cost of living and the lack of affordable housing in Ireland, depicting the two old parties as intertwined relics, equally committed to maintaining an *ancien régime* that simply did not offer a fair deal for ordinary people. In that respect, they succeeded in firmly positioning themselves as the centre-left alternative. With the Irish Labour Party still suffering the electoral stigma of being part of an earlier coalition with Fine Gael that implemented swingeing austerity cuts, Sinn Féin simply swept in and supplanted them. Crucially, they were also Ireland's liberal option. For rapidly secularising Ireland, with a young, highly educated electorate, the party's clear positions on climate change, feminism and gay rights – issues they had previously championed in Northern Ireland – provided an additional point of difference from the other parties. But their surge was not simply about younger people. While enjoying strong support from young people under the age of thirty-four, the party was the top choice for voters in the 35–49 age cohort, the classic 'squeezed middle' of hard-pressed working parents with caring responsibilities.[8]

Sinn Féin's growth in southern politics had been slow and uneven, but in 2018 Gerry Adams relinquished the leadership of Sinn Féin, after serving as the party's president for thirty-four years, paving the way for a transfer of power in the Republican movement. There is little doubt this change earned the party a fresh hearing with southern voters.

Demonised by the British press, and too easy to portray as a Troubles-era veteran, despite his repeated (but widely ridiculed) denials that he had been a member of the IRA, Adams remains one of the canniest figures that Irish or British politics has ever produced. He realised there was a ceiling on how far he could ever take his party. His master-stroke was to groom his successor in a way that political leaders seldom manage, or even have the inclination to do. Mary Lou McDonald, a charismatic and likeable Dubliner, struck a chord with southern voters. She was a political professional with a clean slate. Unconnected to her party's militant past, she brilliantly articulated the frustrations of ordinary families around the economic inequalities blighting modern Ireland. As a vignette, a video of her first speech in the Dáil following the election garnered 2 million hits online.[9]

In a last hurrah, Fianna Fáil teamed up with Fine Gael in an unprecedented coalition to freeze out Sinn Féin. Even then, the two grand old parties did not have the numbers and needed the Greens' support. Yet the prospect of Sinn Féin finally entering government, so long a theoretical prospect that the main parties could safely ignore, is no longer so. The question seems not 'if' but 'when'. Every opinion poll since the election has shown the same basic pattern, with

Fianna Fáil bleeding support, both to their coalition part-
ners, Fine Gael, and to Sinn Féin, as a generation of voters
for whom the Troubles effectively ended before they were
born remain unperturbed by columnists in Dublin's stuffy,
centre-right newspapers rehashing warnings about the party's historical connections to the IRA. For southern voters,
Sinn Féin has been demystified.

So, if all this represents a paradigm shift in Dublin, with
Sinn Féin on the cusp of becoming a permanent feature of
the governing equation, what does that mean for Irish unity?
Most obviously, it injects new pace and commitment into the
issue, moving it from the theoretical, emotional and abstract,
to the rational, practical and immediate. There is no hiding
place for any of the other Irish parties now. While the current
Taoiseach, Micheál Martin, remains deeply unenthusiastic,
his deputy, the Tánaiste Leo Varadkar (who succeeds Martin
as Taoiseach in 2022 under the terms of their coalition deal),
has begun positioning his Fine Gael party. He told delegates
at his party's ard fheis in June 2021 that they needed to develop their own vision of Irish unity and that they should even
establish a party organisation in Northern Ireland (after
Fianna Fáil did something similar, forming a partnership
with the SDLP in February 2019).[10] Trowelling on the anti-Sinn
Féin invective, he told them: 'We know the crude vision

espoused by Sinn Féin, it's not an inclusive one – a cold form of republicanism, socialist, narrow nationalism, protectionist, anti-British, euro-critical, ourselves alone, 50 per cent plus one and nobody else is needed. That is not a 21st-century vision.'

In Varadkar's view, unification must not be the annexation of Northern Ireland: 'It means something more, a new state designed together, a new constitution and one that reflects the diversity of a bi-national or multi-national state in which almost a million people are British. Like the New South Africa, a rainbow nation, not just orange and green.'

Perhaps Dublin is starting to believe that the reunification of the country is now taking form, after being a vaporous ambition since partition. The 'Nordies' have arrived and having stopped them at the gates by forming a loveless coalition, Fianna Fáil and Fine Gael are beginning to accept that sooner or later Sinn Féin will simply smash it down. This does not mean, however, that they have a monopoly on the process of unifying the country, nor what happens afterwards. (After all, the revolutionary fervour of Republicans in the 1916–22 period did not stop more reactionary forces then dominating the new Irish state.) There are, and should be, different narratives about how Irish unity comes about, and a series of competing visions about what a 32-county, united, single Irish state looks like.

The Good Friday Agreement guarantees a referendum can take place when there is demonstrable support for one in Northern Ireland. It requires that Britain is prepared to 'sell', and that Ireland is willing to 'buy'. What Sinn Féin's recent surge represents is the locking in of a sequence that starts to make this possible.

CHAPTER FIVE

PUTTING AWAY THE CULTURE CLUBS

While peace may have broken out on the streets of Northern Ireland over the past two decades, another war is still raging. As political leaders struggle to deal with the aftermath of past conflict, history and symbols are these days used as substitutes for bombs and bullets. Flags, marches and even the naming of a children's park have been weaponised in a game of cultural one-upmanship that leaves any onlooker from outside Northern Ireland wondering if people there have taken leave of their senses.

But this is the natural residue of the legacy of Northern Ireland's sectarian strife, where one community has enjoyed and misused a position of power for so long and where the British state has chosen to allow that to happen. As a result, the cultures of Catholic–Nationalists and

Protestant–Unionists are often mutually exclusive, used as cudgels – culture clubs – to bash the other side. While the Irish speak Gaelic as a means of connecting to their ancient history, Unionists have adopted the cause of Ulster-Scots dialect to show that they, too, have their own separate culture and traditions. While Nationalists paint gable-end murals of their heroes and martyrs, Unionists paint the kerbstones red, white and blue.

But here's the thing. The differences between Northern Ireland's communities, significant and often rancorous though they are, are more surmountable than many of the cultural differences that now divide Unionists from the mother country. Social attitudes in Northern Ireland exist in a parallel universe to the rest of the UK. Indeed, Protestant–Unionists arguably have more in common with conservative Catholics than they have with mainstream British public opinion these days. So much so, in fact, that there were anecdotal reports that some Catholics voted for the Democratic Unionists in the 2016 assembly elections because of their staunch opposition to same-sex marriage.

'More British than the British' used to be the phrase that summed up the bowler-hatted Orangemen; and indeed they were. But that phrase relies on notions of Britishness being static. They are not, and if historical bonds of mutual affection and tradition are what have held Northern Ireland in place hitherto, then these ties are now gossamer-thin. This point is brought home again and again. On many social issues Northern Ireland and mainland Britain exist in parallel worlds, with Unionists quietly relieved that some British norms do not apply.

Indeed, it took the House of Commons to vote to extend provisions for both same-sex marriage and abortion to Northern Ireland in July 2019, during the hiatus in which the assembly was mothballed over the fallout from the Renewable Heat Incentive (RHI) scandal.[1] Neither measure had hitherto been legal in Northern Ireland, a position that most Unionists were quite happy to see maintained in perpetuity.

There was also the Ashers bakery case. The refusal of a Belfast bakery to make a so-called gay cake celebrating the parliamentary vote to legislate for same-sex marriage in 2014 turned into a surreal – and faintly comical – human rights issue. At the nub of it was the question of whether a bakery owned and managed by a family of Christian evangelicals should be compelled to decorate a cake with a gay rights message on it for a gay customer, even if it contravened their strongly held religious convictions. As the *Belfast Telegraph* explained: 'He [the plaintiff, Mr Gareth Lee] was seeking a cake depicting *Sesame Street* characters Bert and Ernie below the motto "Support Gay Marriage" for an event to mark International Day Against Homophobia.'[2]

The refusal of the bakery to proceed with the order throws into sharp relief the fact that divisions in Northern Ireland are not neatly confined to whether you favour a united Ireland or not, or to which Christian denomination you belong, but between tradition and modernity in what is a deeply culturally conservative place.

Initially, the bakery's owners, Daniel and Amy McArthur, were found to have discriminated against Mr Lee, with a High Court appeal in 2016 again finding in his favour. Lord Chief Justice Sir Declan Morgan rejected the family's concerns about freedom of conscience, saying: 'The fact that a baker provides a cake for a particular team or portrays witches on a Halloween cake does not indicate any support for either.' However, a later appeal to the Supreme Court in October 2018 overturned the earlier judgment, with the justices finding unanimously in the defendants' favour.[3] 'I know a lot of people will be glad to hear this ruling today,' Daniel McArthur stated outside court, 'because [it] protects freedom of speech and freedom of conscience for everyone.' The plaintiff, Gareth Lee, responded: 'To me, this was never about conscience or a statement. All I wanted to do was to order a cake in a shop.' An appeal to the European Court of Human Rights has been lodged.

The case is slightly anomalous in terms of Northern Ireland's culture wars. For starters, it did not overtly involve the political parties, while many conservative Catholics will have been rooting for the McArthur family, conscious, perhaps, that any move in law to curtail freedom of conscience has deep implications for them as well.

The more familiar cultural flashpoints concern the past, particularly what is remembered, celebrated or even venerated. In such a historically aware and divided society, sensitivities are everywhere. Indeed, 'one man's terrorist is another man's freedom fighter' is a concept that has never been more apposite.

Back in 2001, Newry and Mourne District Council named a small, nondescript children's play park in Newry after Raymond McCreesh, a 24-year-old native of nearby Camlough in County Armagh who died in 1981. He was the third Republican to perish on hunger strike in the Maze prison, dying after sixty-one days. He had been gaoled four years earlier for IRA membership, attempted murder and possession of a rifle used in the mass shooting of Protestant workers in the notorious Kingsmill massacre, in which ten Protestant workmen were pulled over in their van and shot dead by the IRA. Unionist councillors and campaigners in the area fought to have the name of the park changed and, as ever with these issues, a seemingly endless process to facilitate complaints, appeals and counter-appeals followed.

In 2008, Northern Ireland's Equality Commission called on the council to begin an equalities impact assessment into the naming of the park. Then, in 2012, Sinn Féin and SDLP councillors in the heavily Nationalist area decided to keep the park named after McCreesh. Two years later, the Equality Commission ruled that the naming was in breach of the council's own equality policy and recommended it review its decision. The council submitted a further report to the Equality Commission, voted to keep the name and the commission decided to take no further action. Then, in the face of legal action by the mother of one of the victims of the Kingsmill massacre, 88-year-old Bea Worton, the Equality Commission changed its mind and called for the council to discuss and vote upon the issue again. In June 2016, it advised the council that 'to ensure transparency, the council debate and vote on this issue should be conducted in public and properly recorded and that councillors should be provided with a qualitative analysis of the consultation responses prior to that debate and vote'.

Quite how many other parks across the United Kingdom are named after such forensic 'qualitative analysis' is moot; alas, it is an everyday case of Northern Ireland's circuitous decision-making. When all is said and done, we are talking about a single children's playground. Yet the importance of culture and what the discordant communities of Northern Ireland choose to commemorate – or cultivate resentments about – take precedence. The process becomes an immovable obstacle that retains the ability to undermine political progress. (Doubtless it seems bewildering to British eyes to name a children's play park after a dead IRA man, which would be fodder for the confected outrage of the tabloid media.)

But think about it. There is hardly a town square anywhere in England that is not adorned with a statue to some austere-looking and obscure Victorian military figure. Come to that, how many Albert Halls, Waterloo Bridges and Nelson Squares – or permutations thereof – do we have dotted across Britain? Is it not equally likely that Irish Republican heartlands in South Armagh – the infamous 'bandit country', where the writ of the British state was tenuous throughout the Troubles – would choose to honour one of the hunger strikers for their enormous personal sacrifice? Difficult for Unionists to accept, or the British to even understand, but for Republicans it is Irish soil, which serves to make such symbolism highly potent, and thus, commemorating Raymond McCreesh becomes entirely befitting. (Indeed, the process is not confined to the Irish Republican heartlands. Bobby Sands, the first hunger striker to die in 1981, is widely commemorated around the world, with streets in five French towns and cities named after him.)

In their own way, Northern Ireland is not really British for Unionists either. Theirs is more of an associate membership, benefiting from taxpayers' largesse and attaching themselves to parts of British identity they like, while elevating their own identity and cultural associations to greater importance. This conditional attachment gives rise to the quip that they are not so much loyal to the Crown as to the half-crown.

Take Sir Edward Carson. For Unionists, he remains the implacable opponent of Home Rule and first signatory of the 1912 Ulster Covenant. The lion of Unionism. However, to any Brit who may have happened across him, he was the Marquess of Queensbury's merciless barrister, pulverising poor Oscar Wilde in his infamous libel battle. Little of Unionism's very specific cultural identity overlaps with the British. Most obviously, the hyper-religiosity of many evangelical Protestants is seriously out of kilter with the post-religious 'mainland'. Likewise, there was little of the skirt-hitching of Unionists across in Westminster at the prospect of seeing Sinn Féin in government, or about the release of paramilitary prisoners following the signing of the Good Friday Agreement in 1998. Even on the sporting field we are separate tribes. Most Unionists are full-throated supporters of the all-Ireland rugby and cricket teams and follow Northern Ireland on the football field, while the UK's Olympics team is referred to as 'Team GB' – omitting any reference to Northern Ireland at all.

So, when it comes to defending their cultural turf, Unionists have little trust in the mechanisms put in place for policing disputes about the rights of identity. Particular ire, however, is reserved for the Parades Commission – surely the strangest quango in the British state – which determines whether contentious public marches can go ahead. Invariably, these are Orange Order marches – and always 'marches', never 'parades', an additional point of friction with the commission – earning it scorn for curtailing Unionists' 'right' to traverse the Queen's Highway wherever and whenever they choose. Similarly, the Equality Commission is seen as another hostile redoubt of politically correct anti-Unionism, pursuing the Ashers bakery case and failing, as Unionists see it, to rule decisively against Raymond McCreesh Park.

Indeed, Colin Worton, the son of Bea Worton, who brought the successful complaint to the Equality Commission, accused the body of seeking to 'ride two horses'.[4] He added: 'They have come down very hard on Ashers bakery, in comparison to McCreesh Park, but I feel this case is much more important. They initially came out very strongly against the McCreesh name but later did somersaults to conclude that they had no power to overturn it.'

Chronicling Northern Ireland's brittle identity politics would merit its own book. There are some genuinely important issues about how a divided society learns to live together and forges a new shared politics amid the infernal tit-for-tattery. Again, however, British observers know and care little for these nuances and micro-grievances. But that's because ignoring history and hoping the past goes away is a particularly British trait. For the Irish – whether of the green or orange persuasion – history is essential. It links, in an instant, their contemporaneous identity with a specific time and place in the past. Invariably, a victory or grievance. Northern Ireland can no more forget its history – or 'move on' in the parlance of confessional daytime television – than it can forget about the weather. It's just there. Felt by all. Yet it's perceived radically differently.

So, how, then, do you de-escalate a culture war? Can

you? Is it possible to find common ground – a shared narrative – between binary identities that have spent so long as implacable opponents? Or do you accommodate both by trying to split the difference and create the largest area of cultural overlap? This is certainly the driver for integrated schooling. The theory goes that sectarianism in Northern Ireland can only be overcome by making 'the other' more normal and more recognisable. So, if Catholic and Protestant children go to school together they will all grow up happily together, in a spirit of comradeship. It's a cute idea, but religion is a badge of association, not the root cause of Northern Ireland's conflict. Marxist IRA men were not noted for rounding up young Protestant boys so they could teach them the rosary, or UDA types for espousing the theory of justification by faith alone to a bus queue of Catholics on the Falls Road.

For political scientists, the Northern Ireland Troubles were an ethno-national dispute. In plain English: my side want this bit of ground to be part of this state, while yours want it to be part of another. Religion and culture add colour to what is, at root, a question of hard politics. So, if we are effectively going to shut down denominational schooling in Northern Ireland (while allowing it in the rest of the UK or the Irish Republic), in order, we believe, to stamp out sectarianism, then why stop at schools? Why not close Celtic and Rangers Football Clubs too? And ban the Orange Order and the Ulster Gaelic Athletic Association (GAA)? Or tear down the famous statue of Edward Carson at Stormont?

Where do you stop? You cannot stamp out different cultures, nor dismiss the interplay of factors that gave rise to them. What you can do is try to build another culture, working with the grain of what's already there, and hope that in time the area of overlap becomes larger and deeper. This process starts with some mutual respect and perhaps toning down the moral outrage about slights, real or perceived, as well as the infernal 'whataboutery' that plagues Northern Irish politics. However, it also involves coming to a view about which aspects of Northern Ireland's cultural expression are valid and, much more controversially, which are not.

Take the most infamous example in recent times. The dispute over the flying of the Union Flag over Belfast City Hall in 2013 led to the attempted storming of the council chamber, rioting in the streets, a £20 million policing bill, threats to the lives of elected politicians and even an attack on Belfast's Lord Mayor. The issue began with a decision of the council to limit the flying of the Union Flag to designated days rather than flying it every day of the year. And that was it. That's what the whole dispute was about. All that violence, animosity and public money simply because Belfast City Council took a legitimate and democratic decision to fall into line with other councils in the UK and fly the Union Flag only on designated days.

Of course, it didn't seem like a trivial issue to Unionists at the time, especially to their more militant Loyalist brethren. Indeed, within a year of the protest starting, 560 people had been arrested and charged in connection with the dispute. Yet away from all the fireworks and fury, the UK's Department for Culture, Media and Sport (DCMS) had clear guidelines about when the Union Flag should be flown. At the time, the guidance was that there were twenty-one occasions when it was deemed befitting to fly the flag from public buildings. To be clear, these were not suggestions and not meant to be added to as local councils saw fit. These were explicit guidelines.

In fact, it was even fewer than twenty-one. For national patron saints' days, the flag was to be flown solely in the host nation. On St George's Day, the flag was to be flown in England but not in Scotland, Wales or Northern Ireland. And in case Unionists thought politically correct commissars at the DCMS had it in for them, the guidance for St

Patrick's Day stated: 'The Union Flag only should be flown.' Not the Irish Tricolour. As well as the feast days, the bulk of the remainder are royal holidays and special occasions like Remembrance Sunday.

The very prescriptiveness of the list appeared to catch Belfast's Unionists unawares. Since 1906, the Union Flag was flown from Belfast City Hall each day – seemingly the only town hall in the UK where it was. So, it was entirely reasonable to bring Belfast into line with other local government buildings. In that respect, it was no more British than Bolton, Birmingham or Basildon.

In previous times, the issue did not arise. Belfast City Hall was a Protestant, Unionist citadel and did as it pleased. Over the years, as the population of Northern Ireland has altered, the stranglehold of Protestant–Unionist culture has eroded. The row over flying the Union Flag was inevitable as the demography of the city, and, in turn, the political composition of the council changed, with Sinn Féin becoming the largest party. It is a familiar pattern as Unionist hegemony gives way to Catholic–Nationalist culture.

David Cameron once observed that 'coyness' and 'reserve' were an 'intrinsic part of being British' rather than overt proclamations and displays of national identity. 'We don't do flags on the front lawn,' he once remarked. He was right: flag-waving is looked upon by the English as being a bit vulgar and excessive. Better to flutter on the top of civic buildings than in people's backyards. And then only sparingly.

But in Northern Ireland, flags matter. Unfortunately, different flags matter to different people and for different reasons. To Republicans, the Union Flag is the 'butcher's apron' – a symbol of oppression and imperial brutality. To Unionists, the Irish Tricolour is the flag of a foreign country, one to which they insist they have no affinity – which is perhaps surprising (and a cause for regret) given its origins. The green, white and orange Tricolour was presented to leaders of the Young Ireland movement of radical Republicans on a visit to France in 1848. One of their leading lights, Thomas Francis Meagher, brought it back to Ireland and flew it for the first time in Waterford. Meagher explained its significance thus: 'The white in the centre signifies a lasting truce between the "orange" and the "green" and I trust that beneath its folds, the hands of the Irish Protestant and the Irish Catholic may be clasped in generous and heroic brotherhood.'[5]

Some hope. Although the Young Irelanders – like many Irish revolutionary movements down the years – were led by Protestants, this history is exorcised from Unionist historical narrative. Men like Theobald Wolfe Tone, Robert Emmet, William Smith O'Brien and Charles Stewart Parnell – Protestants all – play no part whatsoever in Unionism's self-identity.

Nationalists are more comfortable in their identity than Unionists, whose suspicions about being sold out of their birth right, as they see it, have been well founded as political leaders from the time of Gladstone onwards have looked for a suitable opportunity to give them up as part of a comprehensive deal on granting independence to Ireland. In contrast, Irish cultural identity, in computing parlance, exists on the Cloud. It is downloadable anywhere in the world, a truly global phenomenon. When the BBC World Service ran an online poll in 2002 to determine the world's favourite song, the winner was 'A Nation Once Again', the stirring patriotic ballad written in the 1840s by Thomas Davis, another leading member of the Young Ireland movement (and another Protestant Republican).[6] The verse invited the Irish to draw inspiration from the Greeks at the Battle of Thermopylae in 480 BC, taking on the might of the Persian Army:

> When boyhood's fire was in my blood
> I read of ancient free men
> For Greece and Rome who bravely stood,

Three hundred men and three men.

And then I prayed I yet might see

Our fetters rent in twain,

And Ireland, long a province, be

A Nation once again!

Where Irish Nationalist culture – a mixture of language, dance, music, song, literature, traditional sports and the veneration of hero-martyrs – endures, Unionist culture, in contrast, struggles to keep pace. That isn't to deny there is a specific culture to commemorate, just that, for the majority of the twentieth century, Unionist identity has been inseparable from wielding political power in Northern Ireland. The two have been symbiotic; the state and its loyal garrison people were one and the same – where communal domination and entitlement went hand in hand. The erosion of Unionist hegemony in recent decades – spurred on by the forced equality agenda stemming from the Good Friday Agreement – has meant a reappraisal was necessary. Belatedly, Unionists realised that while Republicans may have decommissioned their weapons, they are still outgunned by them when it comes to fighting a culture war.

This doesn't deter some. The DUP's Gregory Campbell is Unionism's most enthusiastic nose tweaker of Nationalists.

In a long career as a culture warrior, Campbell has criticised *The Simpsons* for an episode about St Patrick's Day, berated the singer Dido for sampling a lyric from an Irish protest song, tabled a parliamentary motion in the House of Commons calling for the car manufacturer Kia to change the name of a car model (the bizarrely titled 'Provo'), attacked the BBC for playing an excerpt from 'Roll of Honour' (an Irish rebel song that had been rereleased in the charts to draw attention to the Scottish government's draconian legislation banning the singing of protest songs at football matches) and was himself temporarily banned from the Northern Ireland Assembly after mocking the Irish language.

Rent-a-quote reactionaries aside, there have been grownup attempts to address the cultural divide. As part of the Good Friday Agreement, a series of cross-border bodies have been created to address specific all-Ireland issues. One of these is Tha Boord o Ulstèr-Scotch – the Ulster-Scots Agency, which is charged with the 'promotion of greater awareness and use of Ullans [the language] and of Ulster-Scots cultural issues, both within Northern Ireland and throughout the island'.

Despite these earnest efforts at even-handedness, older enmities tend to ignite. Literally, and on an annual basis, when it comes to the Protestant marching season, the single most disruptive and divisive cultural event, which has so often resulted in tension and violence. The centrepiece comes on 12 July each year as Protestants celebrate the anniversary of the Battle of the Boyne in 1690, when King William of Orange defeated Catholic King James II. The night before sees bonfires lit across Northern Ireland, with many now adorned with Irish symbols, including the Tricolour, as well as Sinn Féin election posters, effigies of politicians (invariably Republicans) and, all too often, abusive and threatening remarks. 'KAT' ('Kill All Taigs', a derogatory term for Catholics) is a particular favourite.

Again, Britons observing this annualiscd ritual, where several of the most contentious marches are refused permission to pass through Nationalist communities, are utterly puzzled to see night after night of stone-throwing and aggravation, with Northern Ireland's militarised police responding with water cannons and baton rounds. And, while much of the angst concerns a relatively small number of events, this is of scant regard given the disproportionate impact they have frequently had.

As mentioned, contentious parades are regulated by the Parades Commission, fulfilling its responsibilities under the Public Processions (Northern Ireland) Act 1998. Its duties and functions include promoting 'greater understanding by the general public of issues concerning public processions'. It seeks to 'promote and facilitate mediation as a means of resolving disputes concerning public processions' and to keep itself 'generally informed as to the conduct of public processions and protest meetings'. The six commissioners, drawn widely from across Northern Ireland, are appointed by and report to the Secretary of State for Northern Ireland. Unionists would dearly love to see the Parades Commission scrapped. They see it as infringing their historic right to march wherever they wish, usually along traditional routes that take them past Nationalist communities who at one time knew to keep their heads down but who over the past couple of decades simply refuse to turn the other cheek while marching bands play inflammatory songs outside their homes and churches.

The Orange Order came into existence as a bulwark against Catholicism – it's hard to describe it in less belligerent terms – and it is something of an understatement to point out that it predates notions of political correctness. Not only are Catholics prohibited from joining the order (although it's doubtful they would get much out of it in any event) but any putative member who is married to a Catholic or has Catholic relations is also banned. As you would expect, the modern order does its best to finesse this point

these days, citing its purpose as 'the defence of Protestantism' rather than the baiting of Catholics.

Indeed, it was Pope Alexander VIII who urged William of
Orange to invade Ireland in the first place, to clip the wings
of Louis XIV, who was backing James I. Although its numbers are in steady decline, halving since the 1960s to around
35,000 today, it is for Unionists an important element of
the fabric of their identity, and there is no problem with it
continuing to exist. In fact, the order's work in helping to
remember and commemorate the fallen of the First World
War is an important and entirely worthy endeavour. The
sacrifices of the brave men of the 36th Ulster Division at the
Somme transcends their Ulster patriotism, and everyone
should be able and willing to remember their enormous
courage.

Nor should there be any problem with their traditional
marches. All that is required – all that has ever been required
– is for tradition to meet modernity halfway. Northern Ireland is a big place with a small population. There are no
shortages of locations to hold marches that will not cause
friction. There should be no question, however, of passing
through areas where they are plainly unwelcome, or playing inflammatory, sectarian songs as they pass by Catholic
churches. Huffing and puffing about their historic 'right' to

do so does not come into it. It is a question of give and take. The quid pro quo is that the Orange Order maintains its idiosyncratic traditions but stays out of communities where it is not wanted. This is exactly how any contentious event would be approached anywhere else in the UK. (Thankfully, the marching season has been noticeably quieter in recent years.)

Of course, in a united Ireland, the order would, in all probability, thrive, such is the desire to placate Unionists' cultural sensitivities. There are already parades in the Irish Republic without any problems, like the annual Orange march in Rossnowlagh, County Donegal – the highlight of the order's 12 July commemorations in the Republic – which includes representatives from up to fifty lodges from across southern Ireland, Northern Ireland and parts of Britain. The march has been taking place since 1900, predating the very creation of Northern Ireland, and provides an example of how Protestant–Unionist culture can be accommodated in a reunified Irish state.

But it's not just Unionists who need to bend their principles in the cause of building a shared future. Nationalism, too, must show willing. How about a united Ireland joining – or, technically, rejoining – the Commonwealth? Having initially been a member, Ireland left abruptly in 1949 in a de Valera-inspired fit of pique. Might Ireland make common cause with the dozens of other republics that have successfully prised themselves away from Britain in what is now a sort of post-imperial networking club? Is it a threat to Ireland's sense of itself to make common alliance with the auld enemy over diplomatic niceties? This is, of course, a rhetorical question: of course it isn't. Indeed, there is a steady trickle of voices in Irish politics making the case for Ireland rejoining the Commonwealth. Fine Gael TD Frank Feighan is a leading proponent and has pointed out that thirty-three members of the Commonwealth are republics and many of those have a large Irish diaspora. After all, confidence-building must work both ways and if it serves to aid Unionists in preserving aspects of their identity in a united Ireland, then it is a small price to pay.

The former Deputy First Minister, the late Martin McGuinness, certainly 'walked the talk' in this regard. His handshake with the Queen in 2012 during her Diamond Jubilee visit to Northern Ireland was the type of small gesture of normality that reverberated widely. (Fittingly, Her Majesty wore green for the occasion.) Perhaps the high point of McGuinness's cultural diplomacy came when he attended a banquet in 2014 in honour of President Michael D. Higgins's state visit to Britain. McGuinness, attired in white tie, was content to toast the Queen and stand for the national anthem.

In June 2016, he paid an official visit to the Battle of the Somme commemorations in France, laying a wreath for the fallen of the 36th Ulster Division and 16th (Irish) Division. He admitted that as a 'proud Irish Republican' he was out of his comfort zone but thought it was right to pay his respects to the fallen, representing, as he did, all the people of Northern Ireland as Deputy First Minister. His strategy of making overt gestures of respect towards Unionist heritage won him few plaudits among hard-line Republicans, but building confidence among Unionists that their culture and traditions will have a place in any all-Ireland arrangement remains an essential part of normalising relations.

And while culture and identity are potent sticking points on the road to Irish reunification, it is contingent on all those who would see it happen to find ways of accommodating the various, often mutually exclusive, identities. This could see further gestures to guarantee and protect minority Unionist heritage (although Article 44 of the Irish constitution is already robust in defending the rights of religious minorities: 'Freedom of conscience and the free profession and practice of religion are, subject to public order and morality, guaranteed to every citizen').

Alas, there is much more to do from the other side of the political aisle. Unionists were hardly in evidence during any of the commemorations for the centenary of the 1916 Easter Rising – either those organised by the Irish state or smaller community events in Northern Ireland. This was a lost opportunity. The official events in Dublin went out of their way to be inclusive, going as far as to remember the British forces killed during Easter week.

McGuinness's death in March 2017 left a massive gap, robbing the political process in Northern Ireland of both his energy and his personal leadership. He had resigned as Deputy First Minister shortly beforehand, following the DUP's handling of the emerging scandal around the RHI fiasco and, in particular, the lack of contrition by Arlene Foster (the previous Enterprise Minister, who had introduced the measure). But it also spoke to a more fundamental frustration that his overtures were seldom reciprocated. His resignation letter contained a decade's worth of frustration at the game-playing and foot-dragging of DUP ministers for never recognising the spirit of reconciliation and partnership that the times demanded:

> The equality, mutual respect and all-Ireland approaches en-shrined in the Good Friday Agreement have never been fully embraced by the DUP. Apart from the negative attitude to nationalism and to the Irish identity and culture, there has been a shameful disrespect towards many other sections of our community. Women, the LGBT community and ethnic minorities have all felt this prejudice.[7]

The assembly would remain dormant for the next three years.

* * *

So, Northern Ireland's cultural war shows no sign of abating, and the passage of time does little to make memories of the Troubles less raw and divisive. To illustrate the point, I will explore a few examples. At the time of writing in the autumn of 2021, it is after the Loyalist marching season and during a period of intense crisis within broader Unionism, with threats by the new leader of the Democratic Unionists, Jeffrey Donaldson, to bring down Stormont and the power-sharing institutions if concessions are not made on the Northern Ireland Protocol (the deal between the British government and the European Union to avoid a post-Brexit hard border on the island of Ireland and which involves Northern Ireland effectively remaining part of the EU when it comes to the regulation of the importation of goods from Britain).

It is also twenty years since Loyalist mobs blockaded Holy Cross Catholic primary school in Belfast, hurling abuse and balloons filled with urine and, in at least one instance, a blast bomb at children and their parents because they perceived they were encroaching onto 'their' territory. Just by walking to school. (Unionist leaders had little to say by way of condemnation then and still nothing to add two decades later.) The destructive one-upmanship is abundant even now. Every day brings further evidence of how the Troubles are used to buttress the sectarian divide. Indeed, the practice is almost theatrical, with each infraction and its response well rehearsed and predictable. Some of it is shocking in its casual hatred.

Take this example. In September 2021, a GAA club in County Antrim had dog excrement smeared on the goal-posts used by its junior team and litter, including medical waste, dumped at the site.[8] 'Who in their right mind thinks it's OK to target children like this?' said the local SDLP councillor, Noreen McClelland. Indeed. An odd, disturbing tale, but of a piece with Loyalist attitudes to the GAA more generally: there is regular vandalism to GAA facilities, not to mention the targeting of the association's members during the Troubles, when many were attacked and killed.

Then there is the never-ending dispute about how we refer to the city of Derry/Londonderry. 'Stroke City' is one term used, while the 'Walled City' is another. Anything to avoid the binary description, with Nationalists favouring the former and Unionists the latter. ('London' was added to 'Derry' in the seventeenth century when the city gained its Royal Charter. After winning control of the council, Nationalists voted to revert the city to its original name in 1984.) A modus vivendi now sees the local council referred to as 'Derry and Strabane District Council', while the parliamentary seat is called 'Foyle'. BBC reports meticulously use both terms equally in each report.

Tourism Ireland, a cross-border body aimed at boosting the entire island of Ireland's tourism offer, came in for criticism for referring to Londonderry (after asking in an online quiz where the poet Seamus Heaney was born). This led to Nationalist objections. Cue the DUP's Gary Middleton, a junior minister in the power-sharing executive, wading in:

I pity them [Tourism Ireland] that they have to walk on eggshells due to intolerance. With all sorts of challenges regarding poverty and addiction facing our city, the fact that nationalist politicians focus on the name of the city shows a special type of intolerance.

The city is officially called Londonderry. Those who attack government agencies for using this name only expose their own bigotry and narrow-mindedness.[9]

If place names can cause dispute, so can buildings. Residue of the Troubles can be seen in redundant, quasi-military police stations dotted across the landscape. They tell their own tale of past events, but what is their utility today? The chief constable of the Police Service for Northern Ireland (PSNI), Simon Byrne, came in for stinging criticism from Unionists following a report that he had commissioned which recommended dismantling the police station in Crossmaglen, South Armagh.[10] The area is routinely described as 'bandit country' given the difficulty the British Army and the RUC had with moving around the county, with regular deadly attacks by the IRA. As a result, the police station more closely resembles a fortified military base, replete with 20ft-high corrugated steel walls, razor wire and watchtowers.

Byrne had originally established the review following a row over a photograph of him posted on Twitter on

Christmas Day in 2019, with the chief constable flanked by officers in black uniforms toting sub-machine guns. Hardly the aesthetic of a post-conflict society. It drew instant criticism from Nationalists, with Sinn Féin's Conor Murphy describing the image as 'offensive to the local community and utterly unacceptable'.[11] Realising his faux pas, Byrne responded by saying he had 'reflected on the issue at length' and after 'many conversations with both colleagues and external stakeholders' had decided that he needed to review 'visibility, accessibility and responsiveness of policing right across Northern Ireland'.

The subsequent review, published at the end of August 2021, made a series of hard-hitting recommendations. It said that the PSNI in South Armagh lacked 'credibility' and backed scrapping the station as it had an 'unhelpful impact internally on the mindset of officers and externally on the associations of the local community'.

Warning that the PSNI officers were 'unapproachable and intimidating' and reinforced stereotypes of 'a bygone era', the review called for changes to their uniforms and a ban on officers carrying sub-machine guns. Critically, it found that younger officers with 'no lived experience of conflict' had the same regressive attitudes of older colleagues. The report stated quite candidly: 'South Armagh is consistently referred to as a "unique" policing environment that justifies a security-laden policing response. The Review suggests that it is not the environment that is unique but the policing model. This model and outlook is limiting progress towards a community-focused policing service.'[12]

This, in turn, drew the ire of Unionists, who were particularly vexed at the suggestion that some of the public memorials to officers who had been killed in the Troubles would be moved from roadsides and relocated inside police stations. This would 'denigrate' the sacrifices of officers killed in the line of duty and was 'offensive', argued the DUP.[13] Moreover, any moves to increase cooperation with An Garda Síochána over border policing were unacceptable as it was a 'foreign' force.

Indeed, a lack of confidence in policing has become a familiar Unionist talking point in recent years, as the force has had to reform to become acceptable to both sides of the divided community in Northern Ireland. Despite these complaints about, as they see it, favouritism towards Nationalists ('two-tier policing', as the Orange Order had the temerity to call it),[14] workforce composition figures from the PSNI itself tell a different story, with Catholics comprising barely a third of officers and fewer than a fifth of backroom staff, more than two decades after the replacement of the RUC by the PSNI in a bid to address its overwhelming Protestant–Unionist dominance.[15]

Managing this and other cultural fault lines certainly tests the mettle of Northern Ireland's public officials. Perhaps the most significant recent example concerned the funeral in June 2020 of veteran Republican Bobby Storey, a linchpin of both the IRA as the organisation's former director of intelligence and later Sinn Féin's political strategy, and a key ally of Gerry Adams. Covid-19 restrictions meant that the type of large-scale funeral usually reserved for major figures such as Storey could not go ahead. Nevertheless, 2,000 mourners lined the route of his funeral cortège, drawing immediate criticism as well as a police investigation into potential breaches of the restrictions. Sinn Féin's Deputy First Minister, Michelle O'Neill, part of the mourning party, later said she regretted that the numbers present undermined the executive's public messaging, which had been focused on strongly urging people to stay at home.

The PSNI was criticised by Unionists for not bringing charges for those present, including the Sinn Féin president, Mary Lou McDonald, and many other prominent members of her party. Meanwhile, Belfast City Council was said to have facilitated a group of thirty mourners at Roselawn Crematorium for Storey's committal, again in breach of regulations. (An independent report into the matter later found that there had been no undue pressure by Sinn Féin for this concession and that council officials were to blame.[16]) Unionist apoplexy was muted when similar crowds came out to celebrate Rangers' Scottish Premiership title win in March 2021, with large numbers on the Loyalist Shankill Road celebrating their victory.[17] Creditably, the DUP's Gregory Campbell, usually the most enthusiastic of culture warriors, criticised the breach of the rules, warning that it would be a 'bad day' if fans ended up 'in ICU beds rather than being able to cheer their team on to more success'.

So, what does the ongoing cultural warfare mean for the question of Irish unity? How can there ever be a prospect of a united Ireland when the people are anything but? The technical point is that a border poll on the constitutional position of Northern Ireland does not require that hearts and minds are joined in perfect unison, only that the majority backs a change. Clearly, as much agreement as possible would be preferable beforehand, but it is not a precondition in the Good Friday Agreement. The larger point is that while the divisions in Northern Ireland are deep and painful, two decades of power-sharing have shown – imperfect though they have been – that it is possible to work around these divides. Yes, the antagonisms come thick and fast – and repeatedly – but things go on. At least there are no surprises. We know the issues that cause tension and can even predict these eruptions, and with enough goodwill, it is possible to navigate around them. Creating space to recognise and respect different identities is possible, if the political will exists to do so.

CHAPTER SIX

GOOD BUDDIES? RESETTING THE RELATIONSHIP BETWEEN BRITAIN AND A UNITED IRELAND

The Easter Rising, the week-long insurrection by Irish Republicans in Dublin in April 1916, triggered a sequence of events that eventually led to the creation of the Irish Free State and the establishment of Northern Ireland. It is something of a secret history to most people on the British side of the Irish Sea, which is remiss, given it also effectively symbolised the beginning of the end of the British Empire. The total loss of control in Dublin, even for just a matter of days, was a wounding humiliation. If uppity Nationalists could bring the second city of the Empire to its knees, nothing would ever be the same again.

And it never was. The event inspired countless other

national liberation movements throughout the twentieth century. Everyone from Lenin to Mandela took inspiration from the rising. A young Vietnamese man working in a London hotel as a dishwasher watching events in Ireland unfold, as rebels made their bid for freedom in what became the War of Independence following the rising, was moved to remark on the death of Republican hunger striker Terence MacSwiney that 'a country with a citizen like this will never surrender'.[1] His name was Ho Chi Minh, and he would go on to emulate the guerrilla warfare tactics developed in Ireland as he took on the might of the United States' war machine in the Vietnam War.

Events across Ireland commemorating the centenary of the rising in 2016 stirred long in the psyche of the Irish. Memories of Easter 1916 stalk Irish politics. They should be remembered here in Britain too, with a measure of shame and regret for our failure to do the decent thing back then. Irish revisionist history (a version sympathetic to Britain) has it that, by the standards of the time and taking into consideration we were midway through the First World War, the harsh treatment meted out to the rising's main protagonists was no worse than what should have been expected. But tying the badly wounded trade union leader James Connolly, one of the main rebel commanders, as well as one of the signatories of Ireland's Declaration of Independence, to a chair in the yard outside Dublin's Kilmainham Gaol because he could not stand up, merely for the pleasure of killing him by firing squad, was as disastrous a piece of PR then as it sounds now. The price Britain paid for its wanton overreaction was to allow relations with the nascent Irish Free State to fester for the remainder of the century.

A free, independent, 32-county Ireland could have been the UK's staunchest ally throughout the twentieth century. So much pain could have been avoided – and perhaps more radical demands headed off – had Britain kept its word and legislated for Home Rule during any of the various attempts at doing so in the late Victorian and Edwardian periods. Alas, a specially reserved contempt for the Irish meant their yearning for nationhood was unlikely to see a resentful British establishment volunteer to make an honourable peace. Instead, we saw partition in 1921 and the creation of a sectarian state in Northern Ireland. The rest of Ireland was allowed to slip into civil war over the terms of Britain's eventual, messy part-withdrawal. British elites cared little until events in the north spiralled out of control from the late 1960s onwards. The failure to heed calls for civil rights from the Catholic–Nationalist minority gave us 'the Troubles': a secessionist insurgency within the British state, pitting Irish Republicans against the British government and its Loyalist vassals. The deaths of 3,600 people and tens of billions pumped into maintaining Northern Ireland's wretched stalemate seemed to stretch out for ever, until the peace process was encouraged to bloom from the mid-1990s and political statecraft superseded knee-jerk militarism.

What a different history we could have had with our near neighbour. The Irish playwright Brendan Behan once remarked that if it was raining soup the Irish would run outside with forks. But it is really the British who exhibit a maddening penchant for contrariness. An independent Irish state, born not from the bloodshed of the War of Independence from Britain but from enlightened British self-interest, would, in all probability and if properly accorded the respect of a sovereign nation, have remained a cornerstone of the Commonwealth (Ireland quit in 1949). Instead of adopting a position of neutrality during the Second World War, Irish regiments might again have taken up arms for Britain, as they had done so successfully when they were part of the British Army for two centuries beforehand.

*   *   *

Fast-forwarding to the end of the twentieth century, it is clear that the underwiring of the Good Friday Agreement represents a complex web of relationships. There are those between Irish Nationalism and Republicanism towards Unionism and Loyalism. Then there are those between London and Dublin, as co-guarantors of the agreement, and between London and Belfast and Belfast and Dublin. The 'totality of relationships', in the parlance of the peace process, between the parties in Northern Ireland and then across the border, north and south, and then between Ireland and Britain, east and west, underpins the progress we have seen in recent decades. These criss-crossing relationships underpin everything positive that has developed since the agreement was signed in 1998 and will come into play as momentum towards the reunification of Ireland gathers pace.

A good place to start, therefore, is to examine what Britain makes of all this. An Ipsos MORI poll for King's College London in April 2019 on British attitudes towards Northern Ireland found that 18 per cent would like Northern Ireland to leave the UK and join the rest of Ireland, 36 per cent wanted it to stay and another 36 per cent said they 'did not mind either way'.[2]

Three-quarters of people living in Britain have never visited at all, with a further 15 per cent having visited just once or twice. Just 2 per cent of respondents to the poll said they had lived or worked in Northern Ireland.

These seem astonishingly low figures. (In contrast, far more British people have visited the Irish Republic.) The 36 per cent who wanted Northern Ireland to remain part of the UK was dwarfed by the 59 per cent of English voters who wanted Scotland to remain in the Union in a similar poll conducted shortly before the Scottish independence referendum in 2014.[3]

'Not so quick,' some will say, 'the same share – 36 per cent – say that they "don't mind either way",' while just 18 per cent are explicit in wanting Northern Ireland to 'leave the UK and join the Republic of Ireland'. But there is a qualitative difference, surely, between those who are content to live with an outcome and those who actively want it to be achieved. The former is passive acceptance; the latter represents clear determination.

What should we take away from this poll? Well, indifference matters. It's nice to be wanted. At the very least, it tells us people in Britain can imagine living in a radically altered constitutional settlement. There's little evidence of a 'first principles' defence of the status quo in these polling figures, with a fifth of the British public ready for Northern Ireland to go (around 12 million people – just under twice the population of the island of Ireland), set against just over a third who want it to stay part of the UK – and a further third who are not that fussed.

In a border poll scenario, this surely matters. A clear majority of the British public is either enthusiastic about Northern Ireland going or certainly relaxed about the prospect. If you can imagine change, then perhaps you start to accommodate your thinking towards it. The British (read 'English') are beginning to price in that the UK could look radically different in a few short years; whether that's just Northern Ireland leaving the UK or, indeed, Scotland as well. Perhaps, given so few have ever set foot in Northern Ireland, it's a case of what you don't value you won't miss?

Brexit has brought all of this to a head. Another poll for the radio station LBC in March 2018 saw 36 per cent of voters prioritising 'leaving the EU' over 'keeping Northern Ireland in the United Kingdom', the latter sentiment backed by just 29 per cent.[4] And of those who opted to quit the EU rather than retain Northern Ireland, 71 per cent had voted Brexit, with their patriotic fervour about restoring British sovereignty apparently not stretching across the Irish Sea. This generated a telling response from Jeffrey Donaldson, the DUP MP (now party leader). Interviewed by the station's Nick Ferrari about the poll, Donaldson said: 'The Good Friday Agreement states very clearly that the principle of consent means that it's for the people of Northern Ireland alone to decide whether we remain part of the United Kingdom.'

So, none of the British people's business? This seems ironic coming from a Unionist but does indicate what many of them know in their marrow: the loyalty they show is not reciprocated by the British.

Another poll from YouGov of 2019 voters in April 2020 had similar findings: 'In principle, more Brits are supportive of a border poll taking place in Northern Ireland than against it by 36 per cent to 25 per cent. A further 39 per cent responded that they didn't know, showing a strong element of disinterest amongst the British public.'[5]

Broken down into party support, this saw 48 per cent of Labour voters in favour of a poll (21 per cent against) and 43 per cent of Liberal Democrats voters in support (28 per cent against). Surprisingly, a majority of Conservative voters also backed a border poll – 32 per cent in favour and 30 per cent against. Remainers supported a vote on Irish unity by eighteen percentage points (41 per cent to 23 per cent), with even a majority of leave voters supportive of a poll (albeit by five points, 34 per cent to 29 per cent). Asked 'How would you feel if Northern Ireland left the UK?', 54 per cent of respondents (and even 53 per cent of Conservative voters) said, 'It wouldn't bother me either way.'

Generally disengaged, with little emotional connection, seems to be the prevailing mood of the British people towards Northern Ireland. There is no malice, or dispute, and the issue doesn't neatly break down as an ideological or party-political issue. The simple reality is that the British do not understand Northern Ireland or think that it is much to do with them. One other figure from the YouGov poll was telling. When asked which country Northern Ireland had more in common with, only 28 per cent of the respondents said Britain, while 40 per cent suggested Ireland.

Of course, Britain has a relationship with Ireland and the Irish outside of the disputed status of Northern Ireland. There is the relationship state-to-state, but there are few large towns and cities throughout Britain that do not bear the visible signs of the successive waves of Irish immigration that has taken place over the past century and a half. From the time of the Irish famine onwards, the Irish have arrived on these shores in large numbers. To Glasgow, Manchester, Liverpool, Birmingham, Leeds and London they came. Usually to carry out back-breaking work on the roads, in the coal mines or on building sites. Their legacy is the physical infrastructure of industrial Britain. It remains in the patchwork of social clubs dotted around the country. And in the Catholic Church, where Irish émigrés made up the bulk of the congregation until recent times.

It's difficult to accurately assess the number of Irish in Britain, certainly when you include the children, grandchildren and great-grandchildren of immigrants, although around 6 million people in Britain have an Irish grandparent. The difficulty with the census (which has only had a classification for 'Irish' since 2001) is that it asks respondents to self-identify. The fact that the Irish are, in overwhelming numbers, white means that if you do not have an obviously Irish accent or surname, you can effectively disappear into the British population, hence there is a systematic problem with under reporting their true numbers. And given the raw experiences many Irish faced with racism, especially during the Troubles, many parents were keen to impress upon their children that they were British as a means of shielding them from abuse. Of course, if you go back to partition and before, the Irish were not technically immigrants at all. With the whole island of Ireland under British jurisdiction, the Irish were merely British subjects. Therefore, to move from Cork to Birmingham was, theoretically, no more significant than moving from Leeds to Bristol.

None of this is mentioned to imply the Irish in Britain make up a reserve army ready to support Irish unity, and there will certainly be a span of opinions on the matter, but what it does highlight is that the reception in Britain towards Irish unity may be more benign than some politicians expect. The close bonds of proximity, family lineage, mutual advantage and, yes, affection that exist between Britain and Ireland will cushion any constitutional change. It is a strong and enduring relationship exemplified by those who share heritage between these isles.

Apart from the pair sharing an Irish background, the connection between thriller writer Lee Child, author of the Jack Reacher novels, and the musician Elvis Costello might appear tenuous. However, both were at Buckingham Palace in 2020 to receive honours from the Queen.[6] Perhaps incongruously given the setting, the two were also asked about their views on Irish unity. 'I make no distinction between north and south, and I really hope the island is unified soon,' said Child, picking up a CBE for services to literature. 'I hope that's going to be the positive outcome of Brexit. It's hundreds of years overdue.' Irish unity was 'an inevitability', according to Costello, receiving an OBE for services to music. 'Maybe in my lifetime, in the lifetime of my children...'

During the dark decades of Northern Ireland's Troubles,

voicing support for Irish unity, particularly as IRA bombs were going off, would have been a marginal pursuit, to put it mildly. But these are different times. Neither man saw any contradiction between standing in front of the British monarch to be honoured while also supporting the peaceful reunification of the island of Ireland. A portent, perhaps, of how these countries, with their intertwined history, familial bonds and overlapping cultures, will, in due course, make sense of a managed transfer of sovereignty over Northern Ireland. (*Mrs Brown's Boys* was, after all, voted the best sitcom of the twenty-first century by readers of the *Radio Times*.[7]) In large part, it is this renewed amity between these islands that makes Irish unity so inevitable, creating, as it does, a new political space free of the rancour of the past.

So, it is possible to believe Irish reunification is inevitable not in the way that, say, a Chesterfield United fan might hope their team will win the Premier League but in the way a Manchester United fan could envisage their side doing so. It might not happen this season, or next, but the day comes closer. It is, in short, an entirely realistic expectation. Previous form makes it so. As does the determination of those who continue to wish to see it brought about. Clearly, there is little for Unionists to celebrate in the polls referred to above, with the British people sanguine about Northern

Ireland's continued membership of the UK, and a large cohort of British people of Irish origin who will gladly see the reunification of the old country.

The relationship between Britain and the Irish Republic, close and business-like if occasionally strained while never really what you would call affectionate, has still been highly successful in not only securing the Good Friday Agreement but maintaining it ever since. Perhaps a high-water mark in terms of British–Irish relations came in 2011 with the Queen's state visit to Ireland, the first for 100 years. Since the June 2016 vote for Brexit, however, there has been a deterioration in relations.

Brexit was always going to result in Northern Ireland having a land border with the European Union, a particularly difficult prospect given the previous twenty years since the agreement had seen the border all but evaporate, with people and goods travelling freely between either jurisdiction. Reconstituting a hard border on the island of Ireland was too redolent of the Troubles and the frosty decades that preceded them. No one wanted to go back and, from the very start, the British government, in unison with the Irish, wanted to rule this eventuality out.

In the days following Brexit, all things were deemed possible by the new Conservative Prime Minister, Theresa

May, who had replaced David Cameron after he 'lost' the Brexit referendum. There was a breezy nonchalance to her first speech on the subject in January 2017. Amid the pomp of Lancaster House, a Georgian mansion in central London that doubles as Buckingham Palace in the Netflix series *The Crown*, May airily promised to deliver a 'practical solution' on the Irish border 'as soon as we can'. The assumption was that, of the three main political difficulties presented by Brexit – the border, the 'divorce payment' that Britain would need to pay the EU and the rights of EU migrants in Britain – the Irish question would be the simplest to resolve. Over the next three years of negotiations, it would prove to be almost intractable.

British ministers systematically underestimated both the complexities of the issues at hand and Dublin's diplomatic prowess and ability to corral the European Commission and other member states behind its negotiating position. Throughout the Brexit talks, ministers assumed there was a technological fix that avoided a hard border, frustrating European negotiators who in turn accused the British of 'magical thinking', which usually involved some variation of a digital border and 'trusted trader' scheme that would also avoid goods checks at ports.[8] Having ruled out a hard border, ministers still needed to assuage the Democratic

Unionists, with whom they had entered a 'confidence and supply' arrangement following May's decision to call a general election in June 2017, going on to lose the Conservatives' overall majority after running what was generally regarded as a disastrous campaign.

The British position did not hold water for long and David Davis, May's Brexit Secretary, and his fantastical electronic border proposal ran into a diplomatic hard wall. At the start of substantive negotiations with Michel Barnier, the European Commission's lead negotiator, in July 2017, Davis, flanked by two officials, was pictured smiling with a clear table in front of him.[9] Barnier and his team sat behind bulky folders. The image remains a visual representation for the British approach. Winging it in the assumption it would all turn out as they wished.

Not to be outdone in the flippancy stakes, current Conservative Home Secretary Priti Patel (who in 2018, when she made her comments, was languishing on the backbenches, having been forced out as International Development Secretary by Theresa May) actually suggested that potential food shortages, in the event of Irish hauliers struggling to continue to use mainland Britain as a land bridge to the continent in the event of a 'no-deal' Brexit, could be used to strongarm Dublin in the negotiations. She was ignorant, it seems, of the memories of the Irish famine.[10] An unnamed Conservative peer told a BBC journalist that the Irish 'should know their place',[11] while then Foreign Secretary Boris Johnson was caught likening the movement of goods across the Irish Sea to travelling around central London on the Tube: 'There's no border between Camden and Westminster, but when I was Mayor of London we anaesthetically and invisibly took hundreds of millions of pounds from the accounts of people travelling between those two boroughs without any need for border checks whatever,' he explained.[12]

Such displays of crass simplicity aside, there was a palpable sense throughout the three years of Brexit negotiations that power and influence between Britain and its former colony were starting to tilt in the latter's favour. Indeed, at a European Council meeting in June 2018, an inflection point of sorts was reached. For the first time, an Irish Taoiseach found himself condescending to a British Prime Minister in public.

'The lack of progress in the negotiations on the withdrawal agreement has been very disappointing,' remarked Leo Varadkar, in much the same way a teacher might review the performance of a particularly indolent pupil at the end of term.[13] 'We still need to see detailed proposals from the UK on how it intends to deliver on the clear commitments it made in December and March [on a technological solution to the border].' His confirmation that he would be rooting for Belgium against England in a World Cup group qualifying game gave the occasion an added piquancy. Yet on his first trip to Downing Street to meet Theresa May, a giddy Varadkar remarked that he felt a 'little thrill' to be there and was reminded of the film *Love Actually*, especially the scene 'where Hugh Grant was dancing down the stairs'.[14]

Nevertheless, over the course of the protracted negotiations, the Irish Taoiseach started to bare his teeth. The faltering British approach turned Varadkar – the least 'green' Taoiseach in recent times – into a British tabloid target, culminating in *The Sun* calling him 'naive' and suggesting he should 'shut his gob' about the border.[15] Varadkar's other remarks at the European Council sent the blood pressure of Brexiteer hard-liners skyward: '[The UK] needs to understand that we're a union of twenty-seven member states, 500 million people. We have laws and rules and principles, and they can't be changed for any one country, even a great country like Britain,' he said. 'Any relationship that exists in the future between the EU and the UK isn't going to be one of absolute equals. We're twenty-seven member states; the UK is one country. We're 500 million people; the UK is 60 million. That basic fact needs to be realised and understood.'[16]

Brexit Secretary David Davis complained about the Irish government playing hardball, suggesting this had stymied progress. 'We had a change of government, south of the border, and with quite a strong influence from Sinn Féin, and that had an impact in terms of the approach,' he said in April 2018, although the Irish government had not changed.[17] His remarks were brusquely dismissed by both the Taoiseach (as being 'strange' and 'inaccurate') and Foreign Minister Simon Coveney (as being 'way off the mark' and 'nonsense').

What really happened, however, was that British influence was draining away in the same proportions that the Irish were gaining clout. Having quit from the European club, and being unused to displays of Irish diplomatic adroitness, John Bull gradually realised that Paddy had twenty-six other friends still inside it, many of them small member states that had extricated themselves from the clutches of larger countries in their past, just as Ireland had. So, it was not possible to isolate Dublin, and the EU was resolutely in their corner. Partly to defend the integrity of the single market and international rules – and to face down Britain in the negotiations – but also because the European Commission was cognisant, no doubt, that other member states may have similar ideas about departing in future; it was never going to make the process easy for Britain.

Ministers' casual assumption that Germany's desire to keep on selling BMWs to British consumers would be enough to override Irish delicacies proved to be a reckless gamble. There was little cause for British ministers to celebrate. So, Theresa May, unable to split the difference between Parliament and her Cabinet and backbenchers, gave way to Boris Johnson, whose simplistic approach to securing an agreement chimed with the mood of the Conservative backbenchers (and the British public more broadly). They were sick of the whiff of compromise.

In 2018, while he was outside the Cabinet after quitting as Foreign Secretary, Johnson attended the party conference of the Democratic Unionists. He delighted delegates by claiming that an Irish Sea border, with checks on goods moving between Northern Ireland and Great Britain, would be equivalent to making Northern Ireland 'an economic semi-colony of the EU and we would be damaging the fabric of the Union'.[18] With unrivalled chutzpah, this is precisely what he subsequently agreed to in a bid, as he famously put it, to 'get Brexit done'.

The Northern Ireland Protocol that resulted fulfilled everyone's stated aim: ensuring there is no hard border on the island of Ireland. Instead, it moves to the sea, with checks on goods coming into Northern Ireland from Britain.

Unionists complain this creates an economic united Ireland, enhancing inter-Irish trade and strengthening supply chains, at the expense of trade between Great Britain and Northern Ireland, with complex paperwork checks resulting in shortages of goods as smaller exporters find the process overly burdensome. It was a highly symbolic step, courtesy of a Prime Minister representing the Conservative and *Unionist* Party.

* * *

Of course, Northern Ireland aside, there is a second constitutional bushfire burning within the British state. While Irish Nationalism may be one of the oldest continuous issues that British politics contends with, the Scottish variant is also threatening to redefine the particulars of the United Kingdom. Until the past decade or so, it was fashionable to regard Scottish Nationalism as a busted flush, a fringe obsession. Globalisation meant nation states mattered less and less, while consumerism in our post-religious and post-ideological age had consigned notions of popular patriotism to the history books. Indeed, the best place for such fantasies was the silver screen. Mel Gibson's Oscar-garlanded biopic of William Wallace, *Braveheart*, may have generated an outpouring of Nationalist sentiment among Scots when it was released in 1995, but this kind of sentiment firmly belonged on the terraces of Hampden Park, not in the debate about a new devolved parliament, operating within the British state, which was created in 1998.

For the first decade or so following devolution, one might have thought Scottish Nationalism had indeed been caged. The novelty of having a parliament seemed to sate all but the *Braveheart* tendency. Yet political ideas have a habit of emerging from between the bars. And, so, here we are in 2022, still trying to digest how Nationalists came so close to winning the referendum on Scottish independence in September 2014 (obtaining 45 per cent of the vote), before winning unprecedented support in the general election of May 2015, politically obliterating the Scottish Labour Party, hitherto the staunchest defender of the link with the UK, which lost forty of its forty-one parliamentary seats to the Scottish Nationalist Party (SNP). It has only ever recovered a fraction of its ground.

In the Scottish parliamentary elections of May 2021, the SNP came within a single seat of an overall majority in the 129-member Parliament. A subsequent coalition with the Greens gave the pro-independence argument a clear majority and the current assumption is that it's now a question of when, not if, there's a second referendum on Scottish independence. Ironically, some campaigners have alighted on a provision on the Good Friday Agreement that there must be a seven-year wait before a second poll. With exactly that amount of time having now elapsed, Nicola Sturgeon, the SNP's First Minister, is gearing up for a fresh tilt at independence, with some opinion polls showing public support nudging over 50 per cent.[19] If Scotland leaves the United Kingdom, will anyone then care if Northern Ireland follows suit?

When it comes to Westminster, there is an enthusiastic effort to ignore Northern Ireland altogether, and, for far too long, it remained the British state's dirty little secret. Indeed, until direct rule was imposed in 1972, as the place literally went up in smoke, MPs could not even table questions about events there, while the urgency of addressing Irish issues has never held the attention of the centre of British politics. A political career in Westminster is not made by concerning yourself with goings-on in Belfast or Derry. Most MPs are happy to issue bromides about the Good Friday Agreement and fall in behind the consent principle – that there will not be change unless and until most people living there want it. Complex though it is, Northern Ireland remains a zero-sum issue. When it boils down to it, either you are in favour of the maintenance of the Union with the United Kingdom or you favour Irish unity. It really is as straightforward as that.

On the left of British politics, there has been an acceptance that the cause of Irish unity has a historical and moral legitimacy, stemming from the legacy of the demands for civil rights in the 1960s, and because of the sense that Northern Ireland was an anti-colonial struggle. For much of the 1980s, the Labour Party was committed to a policy of 'unity by consent', seeking to 'persuade' Unionists about the merits of a united Ireland, until the advent of the peace and political process in the early 1990s, which saw the party become the most enthusiastic supporter of the Good Friday Agreement, one of the abiding achievements of Tony Blair's premiership – regardless of what people think of his record on other issues. As the party of government, Labour assumed the role of honest broker and overt support for Irish Nationalism was put on the backburner as the party became guarantor of the peace process. So much so, in fact, that Northern Ireland Secretary Mo Mowlam received a longer standing ovation than Tony Blair at the 1998 Labour Party conference.

What of the contemporary Labour Party? Until 2020, Labour was led by Jeremy Corbyn and his shadow Chancellor, John McDonnell; two of Parliament's few undiluted, long-time supporters of Irish Republicanism. This did not go unremarked, with taunts of 'IRA sympathiser' emanating from the right-wing British media and the Conservative benches and a good few barbs from their colleagues in the Labour Party. In his first weeks as Labour leader, Corbyn found himself refusing to condemn the Provisional IRA in a BBC interview[20] and was even criticised for the unremarkable act of sharing a coffee with Deputy First Minister of Northern Ireland Martin McGuinness and Sinn Féin president Gerry Adams in a café in the Houses of Parliament.[21]

As a classic campaigning backbencher, Corbyn held radical views on a range of issues that sit outside the comfort zone of mainstream politics, particularly about the Israel–Palestine conflict. These were seen by his critics as emblematic of his naivety about paramilitary organisations, raising questions about his suitability for high office. While many of his positions were hardly expedient in British politics (such as his response that Osama bin Laden's extrajudicial death was 'a tragedy'), his position on Ireland should not be included on the charge sheet against him.[22] Two factors are pertinent here. First, was Corbyn's support for Sinn Féin and engagement with Irish issues throughout his long career legitimate or not? And second, did it serve any useful purpose? It was certainly the road less travelled during the

1980s, when the Provisional IRA's bombing campaign in Britain was at its height, but it was entirely reasonable for Corbyn and others like him to take an interest in the pressing affairs of Northern Ireland, especially as we now know that Margaret Thatcher's government was itself engaged in secret talks with the IRA from the time of the hunger strikes onwards.

Engagement and encouragement, and, indeed, validation, of the kind offered by Corbyn during the 1980s spurred on those in Sinn Féin who wanted to curtail armed struggle and take a political path. Indeed, without such support, the balance may well have tipped towards the militarists who were content to make 'the long war' against the British state even longer. Like many on the left, Corbyn saw Ireland as a classic struggle for national self-determination against colonial rule. But he was by no means alone. Nelson Mandela may be the safest of safe options for any politician responding to the question 'Who do you most admire in politics?' but he was also a strong supporter of Irish Republicanism. It was an association that weathered his transformation into international statesman. Indeed, Gerry Adams was part of the guard of honour for Mandela's funeral. No British politician or anti-apartheid activist was granted similar status. So, for those who still regard him as a dupe in sympathising with Irish Republicanism, it is only fair to point out that at least Corbyn was in illustrious company.[23]

Wary of being perceived as unpatriotic after the mauling his predecessor took at the hands of the British media, current Labour leader Keir Starmer appeared to rule out any prospect of an early border poll in an interview with the BBC's Enda McClafferty in July 2021, describing it as 'a very hypothetical discussion'.[24]

Asked whether he would campaign with Unionists in the event of a vote, Starmer replied: 'I personally, as leader of the Labour Party, believe in the United Kingdom strongly, and want to make the case for the United Kingdom strongly, and will be doing that.' On the face of it, that sounds like 'yes', but Starmer is a careful lawyer. He did not actually mention Ireland in that formulation. Presumably, he feels he cannot appear equivocal about the Union to British voters (it's a huge negative for Labour in internal polling) especially as he has his eye on half a dozen Scottish Tory seats at the next election – possibly as little as eighteen months away at the point of writing – where championing Scotland's place in the Union remains a decisive factor.

A reflexive Unionism remains the default position of the Conservatives, and they remain staunch defenders of the constitutional status quo. As a mainly English party nowadays, their Unionism is theoretical and aspirational – the party came in a distant second place in the Scottish Parliament, with just six seats in Westminster (losing seven between the 2017 and 2019 elections). They are in a similar situation in Wales, and while they maintain a basic party infrastructure in Northern Ireland, they have no representatives in the assembly. Back in 2010, however, there was an attempt to change that when they teamed up with their erstwhile allies the Ulster Unionists under the guise of the 'Ulster Conservatives and Unionists – New Force (UCUNF)'. The effort was futile: the party won none of Northern Ireland's eighteen parliamentary seats. However, to make matters worse, they lost the only MP they then had when Sylvia Hermon quit the Ulster Unionists to sit as an Independent in protest at the tie-up with the Tories (she was effectively a social democrat and closer to Labour). No similar pact with the Ulster Unionists was ever tried again.

In a recent interview with *The House* magazine, Michael Gove – the Cabinet's leading romantic, Tory nationalist and in charge of the Cabinet Office's Union Unit – said he would like to see 'small "u" unionism', a belief that Northern Ireland is economically better off in the UK, 'becoming the new normal', regardless of people's background.[25] Peter Robinson made the same point a decade ago. The former

First Minister told the DUP conference in 2011 that Unionism's electoral position was steadily eroding and they could
no longer rely on having the numbers to maintain the Union
by dint of a sectarian headcount. 'Our task is not to defeat
but to persuade,' he told delegates, 'but when have we as
unionists actually sought to persuade? And not just by
words but by creating the kind of inviting society which
everyone will want to be a part of.'[26]

The DUP did not take the suggestion to heart, and the
transition from Robinson to Arlene Foster delivered little
progress in this regard. Affecting Angela Merkel's unflashy
style, Foster wanted to get on with the job. In her leadership
acceptance speech, she rooted her politics in the pragmatic,
focusing on 'ideas and not ideologies'.[27] The people of Northern Ireland 'don't want to hear their politicians squabbling
about issues that seem unconnected to their daily lives',
she said. The high-water mark of her leadership came after
the 2017 election, when Theresa May needed the ten DUP
MPs to augment her parliamentary position. Kingmakers at
Westminster, and able to extract £1 billion in extra funding
for their support, the arrangement brought the DUP into
the crosshairs of the British media and political class in a
way they had not experienced before. 'Coalition of Crackpots' was how the deal with May was described by the *Daily*

Mirror, calling the DUP a 'hard-right group' that 'hates' gay marriage while Robinson 'was once pictured wearing the red beret of loyalist terror group Ulster Resistance'.[28]

More prosaic criticism came from political leaders in the devolved assemblies and regional mayors about the importation of US-style 'pork-barrel' politics. The English regions did not take kindly to British ministers ladling scarce public funds over Northern Ireland at, as they saw it, their expense. Not when Northern Ireland was already the most subsidised part of the UK – with a fifth more spent on people there, per head, than the UK average. In comparison to the £1 billion deal the DUP negotiated over two years, Liverpool and Sheffield have devolution deals worth £900 million but spread over thirty years. Labour's national party chair, Ian Lavery, an MP in the disadvantaged north-east of England, described the deal with the DUP as 'nothing short of political bribery'.[29]

Steve Rotheram, the metro mayor for Merseyside, said it was a 'grubby deal'.[30] Just down the M62, Greater Manchester's mayor, Andy Burnham, scolded the government for finding money to 'keep itself in power' by siding with the DUP but not to sort out the twenty-eight buildings in the north-west of England with cladding similar to that used on Grenfell Tower.[31] While former Labour Deputy Prime

Minister and veteran champion of English regional development Lord Prescott used his column in the *Sunday Mirror* to
remind Theresa May that she had told a nurse during one of
the TV election debates there was no 'magic money tree' to
fund a pay rise for her. 'But she was able to shake its branches to deliver £100 million for each Democratic Unionist
Party MP to buy their support,' Prescott blasted.[32]

Nor was the deal welcomed in Wales and Scotland. Welsh
First Minister Carwyn Jones described the deal as 'a straight
bung' that 'further weakens the UK'.[33] Ominously, he added:
'This is a short-term fix which will have far-reaching and
destabilising consequences.' Scotland's First Minister, Nicola
Sturgeon, also weighed in, calling it a 'grubby, shameless
deal' and the 'worst kind of pork barrel politics'.[34]

Ultimately, the DUP's support for the Conservatives
proved to be a false dawn, losing two parliamentary seats
in the 2019 election, which delivered a thumping majority
for Boris Johnson and nullified the arrangement and agreed
the Northern Ireland Protocol as part of his Brexit Withdrawal Agreement. The future's bright, 'the future's orange',
quipped one of their MPs, Ian Paisley Jr, when the arrangement to support the Conservatives was first agreed in 2017,
seemingly unaware it was a defunct marketing slogan from
a company that had ceased to exist.[35] As a metaphor for the

state of Unionism, it took some beating. Out of time and place, reciting yesterday's slogans.

It was all a long way from the mid-1990s, when the Ulster Unionist Party propped up John Major's government after losing its small parliamentary majority in 1996. This came at a crucial stage of the peace and political process, allowing them to exert a blocking influence that saw the Provisional IRA rescind its ceasefire in frustration at the glacial pace of progress, while an uneasy stalemate descended in the run-up to the 1997 general election. Things got moving once Labour won the election with a landslide. Labour has not been immune from making similar overtures towards Unionists itself, however. James Callaghan's government was kept afloat in the late 1970s by bartering tactical deals with minority parties, including the Ulster Unionists. At the tail end of the 2010 election campaign – and before David Cameron made a deal with the Liberal Democrats – there was a view in Labour circles that the Democratic Unionists could be persuaded to break for Labour in the result of a hung parliament. Gordon Brown, in his capacity as leader of the Labour Party, wrote to Peter Robinson (after the civil service vetoed it coming from him in his role as Prime Minister) guaranteeing that Northern Ireland's block grant would be left intact. Robinson was keen to present himself as a leader who could wangle the best deal from Westminster and had requested written confirmation from Brown so he could use the letter as a prop for a televised leaders' debate.

* * *

The past few years have been corrosive for Northern Ireland's place in the Union. Relations between Britain and Ireland and those within Northern Ireland have been strained and tested. Brexit has ensured that divisions have emerged between London and Dublin, publicly and repeatedly, while in Belfast the assembly was mothballed for three years following the row about the Renewable Heat Incentive scandal and Martin McGuinness's death. Theresa May's description of 'our precious Union' and Boris Johnson's invocation of 'our four nations' will come as cold comfort to many Unionists, who will surely sense that they are out of sight and mind in Westminster, and, perhaps more importantly, beyond the affections of ordinary Britons. The United Kingdom is changing, not just with the possibility of Northern Ireland leaving via the border poll guarantee that sits in the Good Friday Agreement but with Scotland inching closer towards the exit. No political leader seems equal to the task of pushing back against these trends. The English regions demand further devolution, tired of the concentration of power and wealth in London, while even Wales has seen a surge in popular support for independence, with one poll suggesting 39 per cent now favour a break from the UK.[36]

If we accept that the Good Friday Agreement makes Northern Ireland's position in the Union contestable, with a clear mechanism in a border poll to confirm that proposition; and that Britain has no selfish strategic or economic interest in maintaining its presence longer than it has to; and that the economic logic of a single Irish state is compelling; and that demographic changes are tilting the balance making consent for unity more likely in the future; and that southern Irish voters are less and less reluctant to take on their once-problematic northern siblings, then it is time to prepare for change.

British and Irish political elites need to be honest in accepting that Irish unity is the most probable long-term settlement; indeed, the best outcome for both the Irish *and* the British people. They need to take charge of the emerging discussion and should overcome their historical inclination to kick the can down the road. If there is no desire for Northern Ireland to become an integral part of the United

Kingdom – and there is not one jot of proof that there is – then the only plausible position is to manage the transition to a united Ireland. This can be achieved while honouring the Good Friday Agreement and the principle of consent. Moreover, we, the British public, are entitled to an opinion on Northern Ireland. Discussing and agreeing the shape of the British state is not a conversation reserved for a declining number of Unionists in Northern Ireland. Not when the territory they would have us maintain remains heavily disputed and not while it costs British taxpayers £10 billion a year. The radically improved relationship between Britain and Ireland, and within Northern Ireland, notwithstanding the periodic difficulties that throws up, now sets the backdrop that should allow that conversation to take place.

CHAPTER SEVEN

HOW NORTHERN IRELAND WILL LEAVE THE UK

According to the Office for National Statistics, there are 609,000 people aged ninety and above living in the UK.[1] Of that number, around 15,120 are centenarians, 350 of whom live in Northern Ireland.[2] During that time span, they will have lived through tumultuous change. The aftermath of the First World War. Then the Second World War. The Great Depression. The first human being to walk on the moon. They will have seen empires come and go, entire states come into being before morphing into something else. Fashions in clothes, or ideas, will have changed and come back around again. Among the rich tapestry of their lives, meriting much less attention than many of the key global events they will have witnessed, remains one simple fact. They will have been born before Northern Ireland came into existence in 1921.

At the time of writing, we are in the autumn of Northern Ireland's centenary year. Covid-19 restrictions mean it has passed with little fanfare. This is an obvious disappointment for Unionists but pales against the fallout from their ardent support for Brexit. Simmering tensions in Loyalist communities over the Northern Ireland Protocol have spilled over into sinister street protests throughout 2021, with gangs of young Loyalists throwing petrol bombs at flashpoint areas in Belfast, and ripping up copies of the Good Friday Agreement in opposition to the Northern Ireland Protocol, as they let their rhetoric and theatrics get the better of them. Older men from the paramilitaries orchestrate proceedings from the wings, while Unionist politicians mutter darkly about the consequences that will follow if the protocol is not junked.

The Democratic Unionists are taking the blame for trusting Boris Johnson when he told their party conference in 2018 that he would not countenance a border in the Irish Sea to avoid a hard land border, before promptly negotiating exactly that, with a casual disregard for the implications that Unionist politicians would end up dealing with. For their swelling band of critics, it has merely served to underline the

DUP's naivety in trusting him in the first place. As a result, the party is leaching support, both to the (slightly) more liberal Ulster Unionists and to the (slightly) more hard-line Traditional Unionist Voice, splitting the Unionist vote and opening up the prospect that Sinn Féin will emerge as the largest party in the next assembly elections, scheduled for May 2022, symbolically taking the job of First Minister in the process. So, some centenary.

Indisputably, Northern Ireland remains part of the United Kingdom, but we are a long way from the 'Protestant state' that Sir James Craig, Northern Ireland's first Prime Minister, once boasted he would create a century ago. Its place in the UK now hangs by a gossamer thread. The core of my argument in the first edition of this book remains intact. A combination of British indifference towards Northern Ireland, and the changing composition of its society, measured in demographics and electoral results, together with profound changes in southern Ireland, in terms of the declining influence of the Catholic Church and the remarkable dynamism of the country's economy, added to centrifugal forces in the British state that might see Scotland vote to leave the Union in the next few years, means that we will reach a point when a border poll becomes inevitable and a majority supporting Irish unity rather than remaining part of Britain will prevail.

No wonder, then, that Unionists feel assailed by events beyond their control and have retreated to a laager mentality, refusing to engage with these realities or plan an alternative course to bolster their political position. In stark contrast, Nationalists are confident that the future belongs to them and can sense that a united Ireland is at last a real prospect. This is perhaps an oversimplification, but this has very much been the tenor of the political debate these past few years. In terms of optimism, there is now a palpable imbalance between Unionists and Nationalists. Especially as Irish unity is becoming a received opinion in many quarters beyond Northern Ireland. It must be in order to make it onto the front cover of *The Economist* in the form of a map of Ireland, with a zipper representing the border.[3] Back in February 2020, the newspaper, which serves as a bulletin board of the international political and corporate elite, claimed that:

> Scottish independence has grabbed headlines since Brexit, but it is time to recognise the chances of a different secession from the United Kingdom. Sinn Féin's success at the [Irish general] election [in February 2020] is just the latest reason to think that a united Ireland within a decade or so is a real – and growing – possibility.

It is not *The Economist*'s style to offer endorsements; it speculates intelligently on what is likely to happen, explores whether it is feasible and then tells readers if they should be concerned or not. An illustration, perhaps, that Irish unity is now being 'priced in' by policy makers and business leaders. We will continue to see animated discussions about the timeline, but the direction of travel is increasingly accepted. There is a magnetic effect pulling us towards a border poll on Northern Ireland's constitutional status and an ever-widening body of opinion is becoming accustomed to that reality. Indeed, *The Economist*'s speculations are of a piece with other coverage in the British and international media in recent times, which has a similar tone, with august publications alerting their readerships that change is likely.

This type of opinion-forming is important in seasoning the issue, thus familiarising and normalising the concept among political opinion formers. Of course, you do not have to accept the inevitability of Irish unity to concede the point that the issue has now undoubtedly escaped from its traditional silo and out into the centre of the political debate. No longer the preserve of Republican idealists, or old men in the backrooms of pubs lilting 'The Dying Rebel', there is now constant chatter about the prospect (Unionist-leaning columnists in the Belfast and Dublin media seemingly talk about little else), notwithstanding the fact there is much work and discussion ahead. Indeed, Northern Ireland's future becomes part of a wider narrative around the constitutional disintegration of the UK, as Scottish secessionists prepare for a second tilt at independence.[4] Campaigners were five percentage points from winning last time around and it's hard to underscore just how lackadaisical British politics has been about what happened in the autumn of 2014. Now, with a reasoned desire to repeat the exercise, given 62 per cent of Scots wanted to remain in the European Union but have been dragged out by English votes, they have a renewed case. In this context, Irish unity might seem small beer in comparison to 'losing' Scotland.

Another thing that has changed is that the issue of unification now transcends Irish Republicanism and in the process has become 'de-Shinnerised'.[5] Other voices are coming to the fore. In January 2020, nearly 1,500 people from across the broadest swathe of Irish Nationalist opinion gathered at the Waterfront Hall in Belfast for an event entitled 'Beyond Brexit'.[6] It included not only Sinn Féin and the SDLP but Irish parties, including Fianna Fáil and Fine Gael, Irish Labour, trade union speakers and, crucially, representatives of 'civic' Nationalism – campaigners from a range of professional and community backgrounds who all sense that the unification of the country is the natural response to Brexit. It was probably the most important political gathering in Ireland for a generation. Having been energised by Brexit, many of those in attendance were also frustrated by the limitations of the devolved institutions and the antagonistic attitude of the Paleo-Unionist DUP, where cultural one-upmanship has become an end in itself. Without rancour or chauvinism, these are voices from outside the usual political milieu talking about how their rights and prospects are better served in a new, all-Ireland setting. Several non-party campaign groups have sprung up in recent years, like the 'Shared Ireland' podcast, which seeks a 'respectful' conversation about future constitutional change, and the 'Ireland's Future' group, which organises events promoting unity throughout Ireland, with an approach that focuses on 'human rights, equality and mutual respect'. On social media, campaigners are ever-present, discussing and sharing articles, latest polls and opinion pieces behind the #Think32 hashtag. These days, the case for Irish unity is made via a social media meme rather than by a stirring graveside oration. But this is the acme of modern political campaigning: building alliances with people of like mind, energising an online community and inching the agenda forward. Tellingly, there is little by way of direct comparison emanating from within Unionism.

Perhaps the most interesting voice to discuss Irish unity in recent times is also the most surprising. 'As soon as that decision is taken [a vote for Irish unity], every democrat will have to accept that decision.'[7] So said Peter Robinson, former DUP First Minister, at the MacGill Summer School in July 2018. It powerfully symbolised the normalisation of the debate. 'I don't expect my own house to burn down,' he added, 'but I still insure it because it could happen.'[8] It was quintessentially Robinson; a lurid metaphor delivered bone-dry. Predictably, he was strafed by friendly fire for providing 'music to the ears' of Republicans, as the veteran Unionist politician Lord Empey put it, by speaking out as he did.[9] Robinson's erstwhile colleague the DUP's Sammy Wilson upbraided his former leader for being 'dangerous and demoralising', adding by way of analogy that he was not preparing to go to the moon in Richard Branson's space shuttle 'because I have no intention of ending up there'.

Accepting that Irish unity is plausible, regardless of whether Unionists ever want to see it happen, is merely the logical conclusion of the evidence before all our eyes. Robinson remains a staunch Unionist and will campaign for Northern Ireland to stay part of the UK, but he also recognises that those efforts may prove unsuccessful in the next few years. As ever in politics, it is prudent to have a plan B. Clearly, Unionists will find it hard to sit on a public panel, or even in a private meeting, and discuss the desirability, inevitability or feasibility of a united Ireland (otherwise, what would be the point of being a Unionist?)

Nevertheless, their political leaders have a difficult balancing act to perform over the next few years, both making the case for the status quo and influencing the debate around Irish unity at the same time. Holding what they have but future-proofing their influence about the ground beneath their feet, whichever flag flies over it. They will instinctively cleave to their doctrinal view in favour of the Union, but if, because of Brexit, this now comes at the cost of livelihoods, then many from their own tribe may perhaps begin to wonder if losing EU agricultural payments – and potentially the family farm along with it – is a price worth paying. Politics is forever a compromise, a trade-off between what you hold dear and what you are willing to accept. Between what you *want* to happen and what you can *live* with. Many people from Unionist backgrounds are already in this space and potentially many more will join them in the next few years.

What is the popular mood telling us about the prospect

of Irish unity? Opinion polls on the issue are irregular, keenly discussed and hotly disputed. First off, few of them have ever predicted a majority for Irish unity. Many now paint a picture of a situation evenly balanced to within a few percentage points. Like everything else in Northern Ireland, though, sectarianism even applies to polling. There are two broad trends in poll numbers about Irish unity, with Nationalists preferring one set that puts support in the mid-40s and Unionists the other, which has it around 30 per cent. The one thing upon which all pollsters usually agree is that their work is correct at the time of asking the question. Beyond that, everything else is moot. The difficulty for any author in drawing lessons from the latest polling evidence is that they are invariably old news by the time a book comes out. I can, however, refer to an earlier representative batch by way of illustrating the point.

For starters, there are two major polls that show support for unification at less than a third of the electorate. Unsurprisingly, these are the ones favoured by Unionists. The Northern Ireland Life and Times Survey, an annual tracker poll of social and political attitudes conducted by Queen's University Belfast every year since 1998, has support for unity at 30 per cent, with 53 per cent opting for the constitutional status quo.[10] Meanwhile, a survey conducted by the

University of Liverpool and published in February 2020 has just 29 per cent backing a united Ireland, with 52 per cent opting for the Union.[11] At first sight, then, a fairly conclusive rejection of constitutional change.

But this is only half the story. Other polls have markedly different findings. A week after the Liverpool University poll came out in February 2020, polling company LucidTalk asked a similar question for The Detail (a Belfast-based news and analysis website) and found a completely different response. Voters were asked if they would opt to remain part of the UK (46.8 per cent) or become part of a united Ireland (45.4 per cent).[12] The remainder did not know.

How do we explain such a large variance from the Liverpool University and Northern Ireland Life and Times polls? Well, for starters, the framing of a polling question is all-important. In the Liverpool poll, respondents were asked: 'If there was a border poll tomorrow, how would you vote?'[13] Given there is no prospect of an imminent border poll, the subject is entirely hypothetical, and without a specific timeframe, or context, or campaign, or discussion of the key issues, voters are likely to respond cautiously. Especially when they are basing their lived reality – being part of the UK – against something that is still inchoate.

Clearly, there is a healthy debate among the stat wonks of

the polling industry about the accuracy of the various methods of collecting data. Do face-to-face surveys (NI Life and Times and Liverpool) elicit more truthful responses than telephone or internet samples (LucidTalk)? Or do they disproportionately survey people who are available in the daytime and not in work, such as the elderly? Given we already know that older people in Northern Ireland are significantly more likely to back the constitutional status quo – and given there is often a reluctance from respondents to voice their real opinions in face-to-face polls – might the result of the NI Life and Times and Liverpool University polls be skewed in such a way?

In evidence submitted to a House of Lords inquiry into political polling in 2018, YouGov, generally regarded as Britain's pre-eminent polling company, argued that online surveying was the most accurate method:[14]

Using quota sampling from a panel of volunteers who we already hold extensive demographic data upon ... [allowing] for more detailed quotas to be set on who was interviewed, ensuring greater representativeness on more variables. Online interviewing also reduces or removes the interviewer effect (that is, people being embarrassed to give answers seen as socially undesirable to a live interviewer).

For argument's sake, though, let us take the Liverpool University figure of 29 per cent support for Irish unity at face value. What is so unusual is that it is barely higher than the share of the vote Sinn Féin routinely receives in actual elections. The party has averaged 25 per cent of the vote in the last three major elections in Northern Ireland (the 2017 assembly election and the 2017 and 2019 Westminster elections). Are we to believe that only an additional 4 per cent of voters across the SDLP, Greens, People Before Profit or Alliance would support Irish unity? Basic intuition suggests that is not the case. (Indeed, the Liverpool poll had 81 per cent of SDLP voters backing unity.)

As an aside, the 29 per cent figure is similar to the 33 per cent level of support Scottish independence had a year out from the 2014 referendum.[15] Of course, that figure quickly grew, ending up at 45 per cent – just short of a majority. What happened is that once the concept of independence seemed to become a realistic possibility, catalysed by the campaign, support among Scots increased dramatically.

Other variables that will impact on future levels of support for a border poll are worth bearing in mind. First, Northern Ireland's demographic profile. The issue of Irish unity is not going to decline in relevance. A poll from Lord Ashcroft in September 2019 showed that a majority across all age groups under the age of sixty-five supported Irish unity.[16] (Precisely the sort of people who are not likely to be answering face-to-face surveys on a wet Wednesday in Belfast city centre.) In that respect, the future belongs to United Irelanders.

Second, any border poll also includes an implicit supplementary question about whether people in Northern Ireland want to become part of the European Union again. This is now a powerful secondary motive for many people who may not be primarily motivated by Irish unity per se. This perhaps explains why polls on the subject that include this context tend to show much stronger support. Indeed, the LucidTalk poll showed 47.9 per cent of respondents would support Irish unity 'as a pathway back to membership of the EU for Northern Ireland'.

Third, we haven't yet internalised the full effects of Brexit. Support may grow among the 'persuadables' (the fifth of Northern Ireland's population that does not readily identify with being either British or Irish). These pragmatists, usually from a Unionist background, might opt to secure the family engineering business by throwing their lot in with the rest of Ireland, thereby retaining unimpeded single market access or agricultural payments. Whatever the shortcomings of individual polls, we should welcome as much serious inquiry as possible, given it's a sign that the concept of Irish unity has now moved mainstream. There will be disagreements about individual polling figures and methodologies – there always are – and about timelines and what constitutes a demand for a border poll, but the fact that they are so assiduously pored over tells us the game is afoot.

Before we even get to a border poll, there is the not insignificant matter of how one is triggered. While the Good Friday Agreement offers a blueprint for bringing about Irish unity through exclusively peaceful and democratic means, the wording around calling a referendum is somewhat elliptical, promising one can be held 'if at any time it appears likely to [the Secretary of State] that a majority of those voting would express a wish that Northern Ireland should cease to be part of the United Kingdom and form part of a united Ireland'.

It's an elusively worded phrase, but its meaning is crystal clear: there can be a poll on Irish unity when there is sufficient prospect of a majority in Northern Ireland – and through a parallel referendum in the south – voting for change. It does, however, seem questionable that a constitutional referendum affecting the integrity of the United Kingdom, not to mention that of the Republic of Ireland, could be called at the whim of a middle-ranking British Cabinet minister. A reasonable assumption is that the phrase was meant to be a distancing measure for the Prime Minister of the day, stopping the question of triggering a poll (or not, as the case may be) from becoming a bargaining chip in negotiations in a scenario where a government needed the support of smaller parties to prop up its position in the House of Commons. (Of course, this is far from an academic point and has happened on three occasions over the past forty years, with James Callaghan, John Major and Theresa May all ending up relying on Unionist votes for their administrations' survival.)

Despite the wording in the agreement, the reality is that calling a poll will be the culmination of an unwritten, but intuitive, process requiring three elements to harmonise. First, that there is demonstrable demand in the north for holding a referendum, evidenced mainly through election results, and perhaps by a vote to support one in the assembly. Second, that the buyer – the Irish Republic – is willing to collect; with Dublin preparing the ground through a process of careful and sustained engagement with Belfast and Westminster to agree and facilitate the reunification of the country. Third, that the seller is willing to trade. Westminster will need to reciprocate Dublin's eagerness, sure in the knowledge that the demographic and political composition of the north has tilted irrevocably and that the number of voices shouting 'Unity!' drowns out those crying 'Betrayal!' The poor old Secretary of State for Northern Ireland – and there have been twenty-two of them since direct rule was imposed in 1972 (and for half of them it was their last government job) – barely gets a look in. This is big 'P' Politics.

The former Northern Ireland Office official Alan Whysall, writing a paper in March 2019 for the Constitution Unit at University College London about what might reasonably constitute demand for a border poll, made the point that although the exact trigger in the agreement remains opaque, there are several criteria that offer a reasonable justification.[17] He cited a 'clear majority in a succession of reliable opinion polls'; a 'Catholic majority in a census'; a 'majority of members in the Northern Ireland Assembly, or the general election, from nationalist parties'; and 'a vote by a majority in the Assembly in favour of a poll'. As he pointed out, 'none of them [is] straightforward'. However, most of these are already in prospect.

Numerous opinion polls have shown support is evening out between those who want a united Ireland and those who do not. *Tick.* Using data from the census and quarterly labour force survey, *The Economist* calculated that 'Catholics are now the single biggest confessional grouping in

Northern Ireland'.[18] *Tick.* The gap between pro-Irish unity and anti-Irish unity parties at the last assembly election in 2017 was just 30,000 votes, while the former now has a majority of Northern Ireland's eighteen Westminster seats. *Partial tick.*

In May 2021, the Working Group on Unification Referendums on the Island of Ireland, again from the Constitution Unit at UCL, published its final report.[19] Established two years previously to explore how a border poll could be conducted effectively, it affirmed that the Good Friday Agreement provides for a simple numerical majority to be in favour of change, the so-called 50 per cent +1. Moreover, it would be a legal requirement to call a poll if there was demonstrable evidence that a majority in Northern Ireland sought constitutional change. What the report accepted is that while seeking dialogue, rapport and trust is of course welcome, a so-called agreed Ireland is not a precondition for a united one. In other words, retrofitting a super-majority clause to the Good Friday Agreement that might require a larger threshold, or even for a majority of Unionists to agree to any change, is a non-starter.

Indeed, such a recommendation would be implacably rejected by United Irelanders, who have the fortuitous precedent of the British government's own Brexit referendum, carried, famously (or infamously depending on taste), by just 52/48 per cent. It provides a powerful legal precedent for honouring a straightforward 50 per cent +1 result. Clearly, campaigners are not aspiring to such a close call. So, the second priority must be to maintain outreach work with Unionists and all those who do not instinctively prefer Irish unity. As previously mentioned, there is not much point in being a Unionist if you meekly acquiesce to the end of Northern Ireland. What is needed, then, is a protracted public discussion over the next few years where the issues are clearly and openly discussed, helping build rapport and predictability. It needs to continue to focus on making a positive case for change, outlining the benefits and opportunities that unification would bring, while leaving space for Unionists to join the discussion at some point. Even if they do not participate, they will at least know what to expect and what is currently being suggested. Unencumbered by the electoral ramifications, it is much easier for 'civic' Unionism rather than 'political' Unionism to occupy a seat at the table. Especially voices from the rural and business communities, given they will be among the hardest hit by Brexit. The conversation should be open and wide-ranging, without infantilising Unionists or allowing the discussion to get lost among the weeds of identity politics. There are only two stipulations. First, there is no veto over constitutional change. Non-engagement must not be used to limit the legitimate aspirations of United Irelanders. For Unionists like Peter Cardwell, a former special adviser to two Conservative Secretaries of State, Unionists are 'not emotionally ready for the conversation about a united Ireland'.[20] His reading of the mood may be accurate; however, it hardly provides a justification for usurping the growing demand for one.

Second, it is reasonable to expect Unionists to abide by the result of a border poll. The principle of consent, upon which the Good Friday Agreement is built, is inviolable. It is also a weathervane. Currently, it guarantees Northern Ireland's place in the UK. If the wind changes direction and the vane points south, Unionists must then honour the decision. The third priority is allied to this. United Irelanders need to develop 'proof of concept'. How will a new Ireland work? What are the benefits? What are the assurances for Unionists and others? There needs to be, for instance, a detailed discussion about what institutions a new all-Ireland settlement requires. There will be a temptation to assume that Stormont should be kept, helping assuage Unionist sensibilities. But is a devolved body, just 100 miles from Ireland's capital, the right model? It would be horribly asymmetrical and lead to all manner of confusion and parallel influence. It would be better to abolish it and bolster local government across the whole of Ireland. It might be useful to consider adopting the British model of 'metro mayors' in major conurbations, providing clustered Unionist communities in the north with the realistic prospect of a powerful executive office.

Next, there is a need to agree priorities around the economy, key infrastructure and the harmonisation of public services and entitlements. Integrating the less productive northern economy into the rest of the country by copying the more dynamic policy model of the south is the relatively straightforward bit. As is ensuring better rail and digital connectivity around Ireland's principal cities. Again, there is much for Unionists to gain from here, and to play a leading role in setting the agenda. Is Ireland to have an equivalent of the National Health Service, for instance? (Ninety-two per cent of respondents in the 2020 Northern Ireland Life and Times survey valued having access to the NHS.[21])

An interesting experiment was conducted recently by a team of leading Irish academics who organised a proxy citizens' assembly, of the type commonly used in the Irish Republic to deliberate on contentious issues like same-sex marriage and abortion.[22] A cross-section of Irish society was pulled together and asked some of the fundamental

questions, like whether Northern Ireland should be properly integrated into a new Ireland or left as a devolved region,
and, crucially, what the timeframe should be for calling a
referendum on unity. The idea of such assemblies is to help
inform the subsequent process and explore some of the
complex issues that sit behind the inherently binary nature
of a referendum. (As a coda to the point, the respondents
strongly favoured unity, but the preference was for a referendum to be held in five to ten years, rather than sooner.)
This approach offers a way forward in structuring the conversation and normalising the issues under discussion.
It has so far been absent from the political debate, partly
because Unionists and the British do not want to concede
that the debate is raging, while the Irish government, wary
of undertaking what appears to be unilateral action regarding the affairs of a neighbouring state, have ignored calls to
hold a citizens' assembly themselves. As an aside, LucidTalk
polling has found 56 per cent of people in Northern Ireland
supported the idea of an all-Ireland citizens' assembly 'to
deliberate on a change to the constitutional status quo of
Northern Ireland' to help better inform the debate.[23] It is
precisely this sort of in-depth, elongated discussion that
needs to take place, and while alien to the British tradition (our referendums adhere to Darwinian rules), raising

the aggregate level of understanding among the electorate about the bundle of issues that are implicit in a vote about Irish unity can only help to improve the public discussion.

Is Westminster alive to the implications of all this? We may soon see Sinn Féin leading the governments of both parts of Ireland. While the First Minister's role is a joint office and there still might not be a plurality of the vote for parties supporting a border poll, to have an Irish government pursuing a clear agenda of Irish unity will be transformational. Both outcomes are in prospect, so how will Britain respond?

At one time there would have been a lot of harrumphing about dealing with Sinn Féin, but I suspect British ministers – coy and requiring choreography to move from their comfort zone – will sense it is an opportunity, taking the position of enabler to an Irish-led initiative. Ultimately, the realpolitik of 'losing' Northern Ireland has no domestic downside for either a Labour or even a Conservative government. There is no electoral price to be paid, no real reckoning with public opinion, no loss of international prestige and certainly no adverse economic impact. And yet there has been precious little discussion or planning for the outworking of the Good Friday Agreement.

Sooner or later, however, the issue of Northern Ireland's constitutional future is going to find its way to the top of the

British Prime Minister's in-tray and the period from 2022 to 2029 provides a sliding scale of possibilities. A British general election by the end of 2024 is a certainty, even if the outcome remains uncertain. Keir Starmer's task in winning it is considerable, requiring a larger national swing than Tony Blair achieved in his landslide victory back in 1997. Eating into Boris Johnson's eighty-seat majority and winning back many seats lost by Jeremy Corbyn in the 2019 election is, however, a distinct possibility. If then, for argument's sake, a Conservative government were returned, how would they approach a demand for a border poll? After all, during the lifetime of the next British parliament we are likely to see Sinn Féin either lead or become a coalition partner in an Irish government. We are also likely to see a tilt in Northern Ireland's population towards the Catholic–Nationalist community and Sinn Féin take the top job in the executive.

Could a Conservative government – as champions of the Union – approve holding a border poll? After all, previous Tory administrations closed Stormont in 1972 and signed the Anglo-Irish Agreement in 1985, paving the way for Dublin to have a consultative role in Northern Irish affairs, before embarking on the early stages of the peace process that would go on to become the Good Friday Agreement. It was a former Conservative Cabinet minister, in Chris

Patten, who reformed the RUC out of existence and, lest we forget, it was Boris Johnson who agreed to the Northern Ireland Protocol as part of his Brexit withdrawal deal, creating the eponymous border in the Irish Sea. (Indeed, a Conservative government held a previous border poll in 1973, which was, however, boycotted by the Catholic–Nationalist population.)

Might a future Conservative Prime Minister, dealing with not one but two major constitutional fires (the other being Scotland), simply bow to the inevitable? Michael Gove's remarks referenced in Chapter Six are interesting because there is no plan, no mystical formula for making the tides roll back. The integrative logic of Irish unity is assured. The promise of a poll is a cornerstone of the Good Friday Agreement – an international treaty – while the economics of a single Irish economy are beyond serious dispute. Add in electoral evidence (which itself reflects permanent demographic changes) and the process becomes magnetic.

Of course, getting Nationalists and Unionists, north and south, Ireland and Britain to sit down and work out a shared future is akin to getting porcupines to mate, but it seems clear, given porcupines are hardly an endangered species, that they find a way to congress when we're not looking. We must not overstate the difficulties in discussing a pathway to a border poll and on into a united Ireland. Even when they have been strained throughout the Brexit negotiations, relations between British and Irish governments are vastly improved on what they were prior to the Good Friday Agreement and its preceding negotiations. Nor should we assume it is impossible to persuade Unionists that their long-term future rests in a new single-state Ireland. As memories of the troubled Irish twentieth century fade, the state they feared being appended to (well, if not 'feared' then certainly 'despised') and the Ireland that northern Republicans hoped to see are illusory in both instances. Bluntly, unity won't be as great as Republicans believe, nor as bad as Unionists assume. In that respect, a united Ireland is not a victory or a defeat for anyone.

Yet the more rational this discussion becomes, the more a single Irish state becomes the only credible long-term solution. And ensuring this discussion is open, detailed and honest simply involves channelling all the energy of the trends that are in play and transforming the political calculation about the best long-term settlement. For Britain, our relationship with the Irish Republic will become closer, more cordial and more mutually beneficial than at any time over the past century. Peace, progress and prosperity.

So, is a united Ireland inevitable? Some say that this

represents a whiggish view of history: ignoring a range of complex variables to make a grand point. Northern Ireland might have its faults, the argument goes, but like the proverbial rusty gate that looks destined to break off its hinge, it just hangs on in there. I think this view, common enough among Unionists and their sympathisers, underestimates the challenges they face. The plain fact is that Northern Ireland simply was not meant to last this long. It was built and run as a sectarian fief for five decades before the advent of the civil rights movement, its brutal suppression by Unionist authorities and the violent backlash that led to three decades of the Troubles. Indeed, many would argue that Northern Ireland simply does not deserve to exist. At various junctures, British governments would have been glad to see the back of the place. Fortunately, we have a binding peace treaty in the Good Friday Agreement that sets out a means to accommodate the diametrically opposed aspirations of Protestant–Unionists and Catholic–Nationalists. But the agreement is not neutral on the constitutional question. The commitment to a border poll is no frippery; it is baked into the deal. It amounts to qualified acceptance – permission, in fact – for Northern Ireland to leave the UK.

Nothing of the sort applies to Scotland. Westminster assumed the establishment of the Scottish Parliament in 1998 would be enough to curtail the demand for full-blown independence. It is clear now that devolution in fact provided a bridgehead for it (in a similar way, perhaps, that the Good Friday Agreement will become a blueprint for Irish unity). Both Scotland and Ireland are small, sophisticated countries with a hinterland in the English-speaking world; however, both are content to take their place in the European Union, with few of the hang-ups of the English. Both are knowledge economies with young, well-educated populations. Scottish Nationalists are showing that the oldest idea of national sovereignty and a people's determination to secure it endures as a rallying point. Like the Irish version, it challenges Unionists to come up with a better reason to maintain the status quo. The only response seems to be to offer the Scots more local control, which, in turn, appears to make full independence more, not less, likely. Even Wales is getting in on the act. As mentioned earlier, a poll for ITV from March 2021 found 39 per cent of Welsh voters are now in favour of independence, up considerably on the 10 per cent or so that used to back it a few years ago.[24] Perhaps it is simply invigorating to be present at the birth of a nation – and infectious?

What, then, constitutes a counter-offer that Nationalists in Northern Ireland (or indeed Scotland) might agree to in order to head off demands for independence? More money and devolved power are already needed just to plug the Brexit-inspired shortfalls. Any game-changing offer would need to top that. But do we know for certain that the English care enough about making it? If the next few years are set to be economically turbulent, and with animosity about the iniquities of the Barnett formula already evident, is ladling even more cash on the Celtic fringe something the English taxpayer will tolerate? After all, they have just opted to end an arrangement with the European Union in which they felt they endured taxation without adequate representation.

In fact, England has its own deep-seated issues. The city-region model – devolving power and finance to mayors covering Greater Manchester, Merseyside, South Yorkshire, West Yorkshire, Birmingham and Newcastle – is redrawing the political map of the UK from the bottom up. Devolution is a ratchet – winding one way – and it is hard to see how it does not lead to the main city regions of England becoming semi-autonomous from Westminster and Whitehall. The process also creates a local political class with a tighter focus on delivering for local people. For England's metro mayors, Northern Ireland, or indeed Scotland, are barely in their mind's eye.

All of which is to make the point that as Northern Ireland slips out of the Union there is no Machiavellian figure pulling the strings and manipulating events. We are merely riding a political zeitgeist affecting the whole of the UK, which coincides with a lack of interest in Northern Ireland from the British public, plus the availability of another viable model in Irish unity. It isn't the 'great men of history' that will cause the break-up of the UK; it is the modest and the relatively unknown. As if to illustrate the point, the average age of the Northern Ireland Executive is just forty, the same age as the current First Minister, Paul Givan. By way of comparison, Ian Paisley was eighty years old when he assumed the same office in 2007.

*　　*　　*

As this chapter draws to a close, let me momentarily entertain a counterfactual, at least as far as my book title goes. What if Irish unity does not take place, either because reasonable conditions for holding a border poll prove elusive, or, if one is held, a majority opts to remain in the United Kingdom? Two things, I think, would logically follow. The first is that campaigners will simply keep pressing for Irish unity, regardless. The Good Friday Agreement provides that no subsequent poll can take place before seven years have elapsed. There would merely be a regrouping around a potential second poll in what amounts to just a term and a half in the life of the assembly. Having waited a hundred years to see Ireland reunified, even the most ardent campaigner will steel themselves into waiting just a bit longer, sure in the knowledge that changes in the composition of Northern Ireland will continue to arc towards the Catholic–Nationalist population.

Far more interesting is what prolonging Northern Ireland's life expectancy means for Unionists. The onus is on them, as champions of the status quo, to explain how the place will work in the longer term. They will need to learn to play nice. Further accommodations with Catholic–Nationalists would have to be made. Take practical issues like recruitment to the Police Service of Northern Ireland. The Patten reforms to the RUC recommended 50/50 recruitment to the new police service. It has never been achieved and Catholic recruitment currently languishes at just under a third.[25] This, and many other areas like provision for the Irish language, would need to be addressed – and Unionists would lose out in most cases. So, they should be careful what they wish for. They may find themselves with a better deal in a united Ireland with everyone fussing over their needs, rather than making concession after concession to Nationalists under current arrangements.

The fact remains that many Nationalists and Republicans are already looking past Northern Ireland. They are content to bide their time until they have the numbers that incontrovertibly show demand for a border poll. Little wonder, then, that there has been a deluge of applications for Irish passports these past few years – so much so that there were reports that post offices in Belfast had run out of forms in the days following the Brexit result. Indeed, no less a figure than Ian Paisley Jr (son of *the* Ian Paisley), the Democratic Unionist MP for North Antrim, urged his constituents to avail themselves of the opportunity, telling his followers on Twitter: 'My advice is if you are entitled to a second passport then take one.' Casually remarking: 'I sign off lots of applications for constituents.' Obtaining an Irish/EU passport might be a pragmatic response to Brexit for people in Northern Ireland, but it still represents a through-the-looking-glass moment to hear the sentiment coming from a Paisley.

But just follow the implications of people choosing to do this in numbers. We know from the 2011 census that 25 per cent of Northern Ireland's population self-identifies as 'Irish'. You could conceivably see, then, a quarter of the entire population of Northern Ireland – some 450,000 people – not only choosing to assert a cultural affinity towards a neighbouring state but actually becoming a citizen of it, enjoying, for instance, its diplomatic protection. This would see the Irish government hardwired into the affairs of Northern Ireland, if for no other reason than to protect the interests of its citizens.

So, yes, the reunification of Ireland is inevitable and likely to be achieved in this current decade. Unionism is in 'zugzwang': the party cannot help but make its position weaker with each move it takes. It is not checkmate yet, but the point at which the game is lost grows ever closer. It is, well, inevitable. The increased talk about Irish unity these past five or so years is matched by a similar conversation about the reshaping of the United Kingdom. The net effect is that a growing number of people are becoming accustomed to the prospect of change. The momentum becomes self-fulfilling.

British indifference to Northern Ireland, the likelihood of Scottish independence and the clear economic benefits of a single Ireland are compelling in themselves, but Brexit is the accelerant poured over this dry tinder. The effects of Britain's decision to leave the European Union have not even bottomed out, but they have already convulsed Northern Ireland. It provides something else; an unwritten supplementary question on the ballot paper when voters make their decision in that border poll. 'Do you want to rejoin the EU?' Northern Ireland would automatically rediscover the benefits of membership. The €710 million a year it has been used to receiving would, in all probability, be exceeded in a deal to support the new Irish state.

Unionists will continue to struggle to find common cause with Britain. They already feel like unwanted tenants, with Britain resembling a landlord that will only grant them a six-month lease. The Britain they know – the Britain of the twentieth century – was markedly different from the Britain of the nineteenth century. So, the Britain of the twenty-first century will be as different again. With ten times the population of the entire island of Ireland, it encompasses a level of ethnic and cultural complexity that should make your typical Orangeman rush to make common cause with your average Gaelic athletics enthusiast. There is far more that unites northern and southern jurisdictions of Ireland than now divides them, socially as well as economically. The divisions that remain feel increasingly surmountable. A united Ireland represents a coherent, logical, equitable, predictable, historically just, economically efficient and entirely sustainable end point in the tortured history of these islands. We have the mechanism to secure it, an electorate increasingly willing to vote for it and two governments each looking for the choreography to deliver it.

We are nearly there.

ACKNOWLEDGEMENTS

I would like to thank the many people who read the first edition of this book and have kindly made observations and suggestions that I have tried to incorporate in this new edition. In particular, I would like to thank Martin Connolly for his incisive comments and encouragement.

ABOUT THE AUTHOR

Kevin Meagher is associate editor of the political blog Labour Uncut and a former special adviser to Shaun Woodward, the most recent Labour Northern Ireland Secretary. He works as a political and communications consultant and has written for a range of publications including the *New Statesman* and *The Independent*.

NOTES

CHAPTER ONE: WHY WE ARE WHERE WE ARE

1 D. G. Boyce, *The Irish Question and British Politics 1868–1986* (Basingstoke: Macmillan Education, 1988).
2 Quoted in the *Belfast Telegraph*, 10 May 1969 (courtesy of the University of Ulster's Conflict Archive on the Internet, www.cain.ulster.ac.uk).
3 Quoted in Peter Taylor's *Provos: The IRA and Sinn Féin* (London: Bloomsbury, 1998).

CHAPTER TWO: BRITAIN'S JUST NOT THAT INTO NORTHERN IRELAND

1 Quoted in the *Irish Times*, 18 April 2013.
2 Quoted in the *Belfast Telegraph*, 15 April 2013.
3 'Interrogation centre had international reputation', BBC News, 10 December 1999.
4 'Undercover soldiers "killed unarmed civilians in Belfast"', BBC News, 21 November 2013.
5 Martin Ingram, 'My part in the dirty war', *The Guardian*, 16 April 2003.
6 'The Murders at the Heights Bar, Loughinisland, 18 June 1994', Police Ombudsman for Northern Ireland, p. 4.
7 Ibid., p. 6.
8 Rachel Sylvester, 'Johnson's carelessness over Northern Ireland is an undeniable factor in the current violence', *Prospect*, 21 April 2021.
9 Chloe Chaplain, 'Former Brexit secretary Dominic Raab admits he hasn't read the Good Friday Agreement all the way through', *The Independent*, 7 October 2020.
10 Eimear Flanagan, 'Karen Bradley: What went wrong for the outgoing secretary of state?', BBC News, 25 July 2019.

11 Jack Blanchard, 'Coalition of crackpots: Theresa May's desperate deal with terror-linked DUP who oppose abortion and same sex marriage', *Daily Mirror*, 10 June 2017.

12 'Ruth Davidson given DUP gay rights assurance', BBC News, 9 June 2017.

13 'Majority of Tory members would give up Northern Ireland for Brexit, poll shows', *Irish Times*, 18 June 2019.

CHAPTER THREE: SHEER MAGNETISM: HOW ECONOMIC INTEGRATION MAKES A SINGLE IRELAND INEVITABLE

1 John Lee, 'UDA and UVF row over money-spinning drug rackets', *Belfast Telegraph*, 5 September 2021.

2 'Protocol on Ireland/Northern Ireland', UK Government, https://assets. publishing.service.gov.uk/government/uploads/system/uploads/attachment_ data/file/840230/Revised_Protocol_to_the_Withdrawal_Agreement.pdf.

3 David Young, 'Brexit Protocol brings huge cross-border trade boost with Northern Ireland exports up 61%', *Belfast Telegraph*, 21 June 2021.

4 Michiel Willems, 'Post-Brexit trade: Irish exports to Britain jump by 70 per cent', *City A.M.*, 17 August 2021.

5 Margaret Canning, 'Reunification of Ireland is close, says top economist Posen', *Belfast Telegraph*, 6 October 2021.

6 'Structure and Performance of the NI Economy 2016 and 2017', NISRA, 21 October 2021, https://www.nisra.gov.uk/sites/nisra.gov.uk/files/publications/ Structure-of-the-NI-economy-2017-Experimental-results.pdf.

7 'Labour Force Survey', NISRA, 12 October 2021, https://www.nisra.gov.uk/ statistics/labour-market-and-social-welfare/labour-force-survey.

8 'Regional Innovation Monitor Plus: Northern Ireland', European Commission, https://ec.europa.eu/growth/tools-databases/regional-innovation-monitor/ base-profile/northern-ireland#:~:text=low%20productivity%20sectors .-,Northern%20Ireland%20has%20a%20relatively%20large%20public%20 sector%20(education%2C%20health,to%20elsewhere%20in%20the%20UK.

9 Simon Doyle, 'Claims of greater loyalist deprivation not supported by statistics', *Irish Times*, 14 April 2021.

10 'Modeling Irish Unification', KLC Consulting, 17 November 2015, https://cain. ulster.ac.uk/issues/unification/hubner_2015-08.pdf.

11 'The Costs of Non-Unification: Brexit and the Unification of Ireland', KLC Consulting, July 2018, https://betaklconsult.files.wordpress.com/2018/01/ report-costs-of-non-unification-book.pdf.

12 John Doyle, 'UK subvention to North irrelevant to debate on Irish unity', *Irish Times*, 9 June 2021.

13 Ibid.

14 Quoted in the *Financial Times*, 23 November 2015.

15 Quoted in *The Economist*, 22 February 2014.

16 'IDA Ireland Announces Results for 2020 and Tánaiste Launches New IDA

Strategy For Next Four Years', IDA Ireland, 6 January 2021, https://www.idaireland.com/newsroom/ida-ireland-announces-results-for-2020-and-tanaist.

17 Quoted in 'Modeling Irish Unification', KLC Consulting, November 2015.

18 'Speech by Peter Robinson, then Leader of the Democratic Unionist Party (DUP), to the DUP Annual Conference, Belfast (24 November 2012)', Conflict Archive on the Internet, https://cain.ulster.ac.uk/issues/politics/docs/dup/pr241112.htm.

19 'Chambers of Commerce increase Co-operation to Support the All-Island Business Community', Northern Ireland Chamber of Commerce and Industry press release, 4 July 2016.

20 'The Economic Implications of a UK Exit from the EU for Northern Ireland', Oxford Economics, February 2016, https://d1iydh3qrygeij.cloudfront.net/Media/Default/Brexit/Brexit-NI-Report.pdf.

21 Henry McDonald, 'Northern Ireland secretary rejects Sinn Féin call for border poll', *The Guardian*, 24 June 2016.

22 John Campbell, 'NI economic cost of UK exit from EU estimated at £1bn a year', BBC News, 24 March 2015.

23 Ibid.

24 'Ireland at the heart of Europe', IDA Ireland, https://www.idaireland.com/.

25 'Foreign direct investment, experimental UK sub-national statistics: July 2021', Office for National Statistics, 19 July 2021, https://www.ons.gov.uk/economy/nationalaccounts/balanceofpayments/articles/foreigndirectinvestmentexperimentaluksubnationalstatistics/july2021.

26 Federation of Small Businesses press release, 4 August 2016.

CHAPTER FOUR: BUYER COLLECTS: THE SOUTHERN APPETITE FOR UNITY

1 James Mulhall, 'Easter Rising relative Sarah Connolly told to "go home" from Centenary event because of British accent', *Irish Post*, 31 March 2016.

2 Andy Pollak, 'Republic must decide what relationship it wants with NI', *Irish Times*, 10 September 2012.

3 'Shared Island', Department of the Taoiseach, 8 December 2020, https://www.gov.ie/en/publication/de9fc-shared-island/.

4 'Taking Ireland Forward Together: The second iteration of Fine Gael's rolling political programme', Fine Gael, 2018, https://www.finegael.ie/app/uploads/2018/11/TakingIrelandForward-R0O2_lowres.pdf.

5 Neale Richmond, 'Towards a New Ireland', paper delivered to Sidney Sussex College, Cambridge, 19 April 2021, https://www.finegael.ie/app/uploads/2021/04/Towards-a-new-ireland-Neale-Richmond-2021.pdf.

6 'Exit Poll for the European Elections, Local Election and Divorce Referendum', RTÉ and TG4, 2019, https://redcresearch.ie/wp-content/uploads/2019/05/378419-RTE-Exit-Poll-European-Elections-Local-Elections-and-Divorce-Referendum-le-Gaeilge-FINAL.pdf.

7   Mark Devenport, "'13% in NI want united Ireland in short to medium term", survey suggests', BBC News, 4 November 2015.

8   Jack Horgan-Jones, 'How the youth vote played out for Sinn Féin and the Greens', *Irish Times*, 9 February 2020.

9   Harry Manning, 'Lou's views: Mary Lou McDonald's first speech inside new Dail becomes Sinn Fein's most viewed video ever with over 2 million hits', *The Sun*, 25 February 2020.

10   'Speech from Tánaiste Leo Varadkar at the opening of the 2021 Fine Gael Ard Fheis', Fine Gael, 15 June 2021, https://www.finegael.ie/speech-of-the-tanaiste-leo-varadkar-at-the-opening-of-the-2021-fine-gael-ard-fheis/.

CHAPTER FIVE: PUTTING AWAY THE CULTURE CLUBS

1   David Torrance, 'Abortion and same-sex marriage in Northern Ireland: Do Westminster votes undermine devolution?', House of Commons Library, 10 July 2019, https://commonslibrary.parliament.uk/abortion-and-same-sex-marriage-in-northern-ireland-do-westminster-votes-undermine-devolution/.

2   Alan Erwin, 'Ashers gay cake appeal told Christian owners "would be forced to express political opinion in conflict with their faith"', *Belfast Telegraph*, 10 May 2016.

3   'Ashers "gay cake" row: Bakers win Supreme Court appeal', BBC News, 10 October 2018.

4   'IRA victim, 88, hits out ahead of play park court case', *News Letter*, 6 February 2016.

5   '1848 Tricolour Celebration', *History Ireland*, Issue 2, March/April 2011, Vol. 19.

6   'Irish song voted world's favourite', BBC News, 20 December 2002.

7   'Martin McGuinness' resignation letter in full', *Belfast Telegraph*, 9 January 2017.

8   Lauren Harte, 'Condemnation after excrement smeared on goalposts at GAA pitch used by young children', BelfastLive, 12 September 2021, https://www.belfastlive.co.uk/news/northern-ireland/condemnation-after-excrement-smeared-goalposts-21549449.

9   David Young and Ken Foxe, 'Tourism Ireland criticised after using the name Londonderry in online quiz', *Belfast Telegraph*, 30 August 2021.

10   'PSNI review recommends Crossmaglen station closure', BBC News, 31 August 2021.

11   Freya McClements, 'North's chief constable sorry for provocative Crossmaglen photograph', *Irish Times*, 7 January 2020.

12   Dominic McGrath, 'PSNI lacks "credibility" in south Armagh as report recommends ditching assault rifles', *Irish News*, 31 August 2021.

13   Trevor Clarke, 'Trevor Clarke – "serious questions for PSNI Senior Command"', DUP, 1 September 2021, https://mydup.com/news/trevor-clarke-serious-questions-for-psni-senior-command.

14   Gillian Halliday, 'Orange Order: South Armagh police report further "fuels allegations of two-tier policing"', *Belfast Telegraph*, 4 September 2021.

15 'Workforce Composition Statistics', PSNI, 1 July 2021, https://www.psni.police.uk/inside-psni/Statistics/workforce-composition-statistics/.

16 Mark Simpson, 'Bobby Storey: No republican takeover for cremation, says report', BBC News, 18 February 2021.

17 'Rangers win celebrated by large Belfast crowd despite Covid lockdown', BBC News, 8 March 2021.

CHAPTER SIX: GOOD BUDDIES? RESETTING THE RELATIONSHIP BETWEEN BRITAIN AND A UNITED IRELAND

1 Donal Fallon, 'Bloody Sunday, ballot boxes and the death of Terence MacSweeney: Ireland's dramatic year of 1920', TheJournal.ie, 27 December 2019, https://www.thejournal.ie/readme/ireland-1920-bloody-sunday-ho-chi-minh-4948034-Dec2019/.

2 'One in three Britons would mind if Northern Ireland voted to leave the UK, poll finds', Ipsos MORI, 3 April 2019, https://www.ipsos.com/ipsos-mori/en-uk/one-three-britons-would-mind-if-northern-ireland-voted-leave-uk-poll-finds.

3 Chris Green, 'Scottish independence: English people overwhelmingly want Scotland to stay in the UK', The Independent, 20 August 2014.

4 'Brits Would Rather Leave EU Than Keep Northern Ireland In The UK: LBC Poll', LBC, 26 March 2018, https://www.lbc.co.uk/hot-topics/brexit/brits-would-rather-leave-eu-than-keep-n-ireland/.

5 Sam FitzPatrick, 'Brits increasingly don't care whether Northern Ireland remains in UK', YouGov, 22 April 2020, https://yougov.co.uk/topics/politics/articles-reports/2020/04/22/brits-increasingly-dont-care-whether-northern-irel.

6 Aine Fox, 'Lee Child says united Ireland "hundreds of years overdue"', Irish News, 14 February 2020.

7 'Mrs Brown's Boys named best British sitcom in audience poll', BBC News, 23 August 2016.

8 Jon Stone, 'EU accuses UK of "magical thinking" over Brexit', The Independent, 26 August 2017.

9 Jennifer Rankin, 'Day two of Brexit talks – and the UK looks as underprepared as ever', The Guardian, 17 July 2017.

10 Chloe Chaplain, 'Priti Patel's Ireland food shortage comments condemned by Leo Varadkar: "People have still not recovered from the Famine"', The Independent, 26 July 2019.

11 Nicholas Watt, 'Brexit: Tory resentment of Irish power within EU', BBC News, 11 December 2018.

12 'Boris Johnson mocked for saying Irish border like Camden and Westminster', Belfast Telegraph, 27 February 2018.

13 Tony Connelly, 'Time running out for UK withdrawal agreement – Varadkar', RTÉ, 28 June 2018, https://www.rte.ie/news/2018/0628/973770-eu-council-summit/.

14 Cormac McQuinn, '"It's a little thrill" – Leo Varadkar can't hide his excitement as he visits "Love Actually location" 10 Downing Street', Irish Independent, 19 June 2017.

15 'THE SUN SAYS Ireland's naive young prime minister should shut his gob on Brexit and grow up', *The Sun*, 18 November 2017.

16 Pat Leahy, 'Varadkar: EU can be flexible in Brexit negotiations if UK "softens some of its red lines"', *Irish Times*, 28 June 2018.

17 John Monaghan, 'Taoiseach dismisses "inaccurate" comments by David Davis over Sinn Féin influence in negotiations', *Irish News*, 11 April 2018.

18 'Boris Johnson MP addresses 2018 DUP Conference', Democratic Unionist Party, 26 November 2018, YouTube, https://youtu.be/FRGBU2TNc_k.

19 Craig Paton, 'New poll puts support for Scottish independence at 51%', *The Scotsman*, 9 September 2021.

20 'Jeremy Corbyn refuses five times to directly condemn IRA', Sky News, 21 May 2017, https://news.sky.com/story/jeremy-corbyn-labour-wants-fair-immigration-based-on-the-needs-of-our-society-10886500.

21 Steven Swinford, 'Jeremy Corbyn sips coffee with "comrades" Gerry Adams and Martin McGuiness in Parliament', *Daily Telegraph*, 21 July 2015.

22 'Labour leadership: Corbyn under fire for Bin Laden comments', BBC News, 31 August 2015.

23 Kevin Meagher, 'If Jeremy Corbyn was wrong on Northern Ireland, so was Nelson Mandela', *New Statesman*, 7 September 2015.

24 Rachael O'Connor, 'Labour Party leader Keir Starmer will campaign for Northern Ireland to remain with the UK in any United Ireland referendum', *Irish Post*, 10 July 2021.

25 Rosa Prince, 'Michael Gove: "This is a rainbow country with a warm, sunny welcome, for all"', *The House*, 13 September 2021.

26 'Speech by Peter Robinson, then Leader of the Democratic Unionist Party (DUP), to the DUP Annual Conference, Belfast (26 November 2011)', Conflict Archive on the Internet, https://cain.ulster.ac.uk/issues/politics/docs/dup/pr261111.htm.

27 Kevin Meagher, 'Meet Northern Ireland's new first minister: A wildcard in Britain's EU referendum', Politics.co.uk, 12 January 2016, https://www.politics.co.uk/comment-analysis/2016/01/12/meet-northern-irelands-new-first-minister-a-wildcard-in-britains-eu-referendum/.

28 Jack Blanchard, 'Coalition of crackpots: Theresa May's desperate deal with terror-linked DUP who oppose abortion and same sex marriage', *Daily Mirror*, 10 June 2017.

29 Jonathan Walker, 'Theresa May signs £1bn deal with the DUP to stay in power – but critics call her "desperate"', *Evening Chronicle*, 26 June 2017.

30 Steve Rotheram, '"It is a deceit to pretend that this grubby deal with the DUP is about anything other than consolidating the Government's position"', *Daily Mirror*, 26 June 2017.

31 'Andy Burnham: If the government can afford a deal with the DUP, it can afford to make tower blocks safe', ITV News, 27 June 2017.

32 John Prescott, 'Theresa May told nurse there's "no magic tree" – but she was able to shake its branches to give the DUP £1bn', *Daily Mirror*, 1 July 2017.

33 'Tory/DUP deal an outrageous straight bung, Carwyn Jones says', BBC News, 26 June 2017.

34 'Nicola Sturgeon and Ruth Davidson clash over £1bn DUP deal', *The Scotsman*, 26 June 2017.

35 Benjamin Kentish, 'Conservative–DUP talks: "The future's orange" jokes Ian Paisley Jr as Theresa May meets with Arlene Foster', *The Independent*, 13 June 2017.

36 Chantal da Silva, 'Highest ever support for Welsh independence, new poll shows', *The Independent*, 4 March 2021.

CHAPTER SEVEN: HOW NORTHERN IRELAND WILL LEAVE THE UK

1 'Estimates of the very old, including centenarians, UK: 2002 to 2020', Office for National Statistics, 23 September 2021, https://www.ons.gov.uk/peoplepopulationandcommunity/birthsdeathsandmarriages/ageing/bulletins/estimatesoftheveryoldincludingcentenarians/2002to2020.

2 'Northern Ireland's number of over 85s rose by 28% in decade', BBC News, 23 September 2021.

3 'Irish unification is becoming likelier', *The Economist*, 13 February 2020.

4 Michael Settle, 'Nicola Sturgeon suggests independence drive could be accelerated', *The Herald*, 15 May 2019.

5 Harry McGee, 'Changing of the guard unfolds at Sinn Féin conference', *Irish Times*, 22 January 2017.

6 Ciara Quinn, '1,500 for Beyond Brexit meeting', belfastmedia.com, 24 January 2019, https://belfastmedia.com/1500-for-beyond-brexit-meeting/.

7 'Peter Robinson's united Ireland remarks "dangerous"', BBC News, 29 July 2018.

8 Gerry Moriarty, 'Peter Robinson has delivered a "wake-up call" for unionism', *Irish Times*, 31 July 2018.

9 Brian Hutton and Amanda Ferguson, 'Peter Robinson's Irish unity remarks "music to the ears" of Republicans', *Irish Times*, 28 July 2016.

10 Katy Hayward, 'The 2020 Northern Ireland Life and Times Survey – Political Attitudes in Northern Ireland in a Period of Transition...', Slugger O'Toole, 16 June 2021, https://sluggerotoole.com/2021/06/16/the-2020-northern-ireland-life-and-times-survey-political-attitudes-in-northern-ireland-in-a-period-of-transition/.

11 Suzanne Breen, 'Just 29% in Northern Ireland would vote for unity, major study reveals', *Belfast Telegraph*, 18 February 2020.

12 Sinéad Ingoldsby, 'Results of a future border poll on a knife edge', The Detail, 24 February 2020, https://thedetail.tv/articles/a-majority-favour-a-border-poll-on-the-island-of-ireland-in-the-next-10-years.

13 Suzanne Breen, 'Just 29% in Northern Ireland would vote for unity, major study reveals'.

14 'The politics of polling', www.parliament.uk, https://publications.parliament.uk/pa/ld201719/ldselect/ldppdm/106/10605.htm.

15 John Curtice, 'Scottish independence: What have the polls been saying', BBC News, 18 September 2013.

16 Lord Ashcroft, 'My Northern Ireland survey finds the Union on a knife-edge', Lord Ashcroft Polls, 11 September 2019, https://lordashcroftpolls.com/2019/09/my-northern-ireland-survey-finds-the-union-on-a-knife-edge/.

17 Alan Whysall, 'A Northern Ireland Border Poll', The Constitution Unit, March 2019, https://www.ucl.ac.uk/constitution-unit/sites/constitution-unit/files/185_a_northern_ireland_border_poll.pdf.

18 'Brexit and Sinn Fein's success boost talk of Irish unification', *The Economist*, 13 February 2020.

19 'Final Report', Working Group on Unification Referendums on the Island of Ireland, May 2021, https://www.ucl.ac.uk/constitution-unit/sites/constitution-unit/files/working_group_final_report.pdf.

20 Peter Cardwell, 'Unionism not emotionally ready for conversation about united Ireland', *Irish Times*, 14 April 2021.

21 Katy Hayward and Ben Rosher, 'Political Attitudes in Northern Ireland in a Period of Transition', Access Research Knowledge, https://www.ark.ac.uk/ARK/sites/default/files/2021-06/update142.pdf.

22 John Garry, Paul Gillespie, Brendan O'Leary, 'What people in the Republic actually think about Irish unification', *Irish Times*, 23 September 2021.

23 Sinéad Ingoldsby, 'Results of a future border poll on a knife edge'.

24 Steven Morris, 'Westminster warned as poll shows record backing for Welsh independence', *The Guardian*, 4 March 2021.

25 Julian O'Neill, 'PSNI recruitment campaign: Attracting Catholics still an issue for police', BBC News, 2 February 2020.

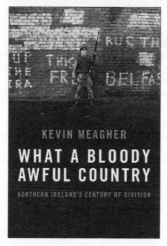